WOMAN TO WOMAN

DOMESTIC VIOLENCE!
A WRONG TURN IN LIFE

DAISY ARNESS MARRS

Cover Graphics: OnyxLenz (Alexis Taylor – www.OnyxLenz.com)

ISBN-13: 978-1-7369079-3-1
Library of Congress Number: 2021915885

DEDICATION

Woman to Woman is dedicated to my beautiful daughter, my baby girl, my second born child, Rikita Desirae Mason. She is a strong-willed woman who, through the circumstances surrounding her life and our relationship, has survived in her own way. As a survivor through all the challenges of abuse, she has become a conqueror. Even though she was not abused directly, her life was impacted by the abuse and trauma she witnessed. Somehow, she was able to pick up the pieces and move forward.

Rikita, although life was extremely difficult, your will and determination have enabled you to pursue a better life for yourself. I apologize for keeping us in that environment for as long as I did. Every day I thank God for saving us, and for giving you the courage to save my life. You have broken the generational curse we once lived under. I pray that you are happy with the life and home you have made with your husband and two sons, my handsome grandsons, Bradley and Brenden. Bradley Jr. I'd like to thank you for loving and taking care of my daughter.

Woman to Woman is my account of the abuse I experienced, and the healing God spoke into and over my life. I believe it is important to share that, although one individual in the home is the victim of abuse, it affects everyone in the home.

I implore everyone who has witnessed, been impacted by, or kept the secret of domestic violence to seek counseling as well.

To all the women who have lost their lives to domestic violence and the many children who have been left behind, you have paved the way out. I pray for the children who have been caught in the fight and lost their lives to domestic violence.

To all the women and men who are still fighting to find a way out, I pray this book helps you along your journey. This book is dedicated to every one of you. It is important to share that, although my book does not specifically speak of the men who endure domestic violence, it is my prayer that you find the courage to seek the help you need to find a way out as well.

To my wonderful husband, Ezell Frank, my Man in Black, thank you for loving me unconditionally and finding me when I was lost. I thank God for sending you to find me.

To my bonus daughters and grandsons, I love you.

To my mother Daisy Haskins and sisters (Doris, Crystal, and Nicole) we made it. It was a long journey, yet we survived. I love you all dearly.

In loving memory of my Aunt Christine and cousin Cheryl who lost their lives to domestic violence. You are missed! I am your voice!

To my Uncle B, thank you for being my rock, and my protector. I miss talking to you, and when you used to check on me.

To my angel baby, we wish we could have had the chance to meet you.

Lastly, to my precious son, Ricky Montez, I love and miss you more than words could ever express.

I pray that one day there will be an end to domestic violence!

A portion of the proceeds from the book sales will be donated to A-Way-Out Ministries, Inc.

TABLE OF CONTENTS

DEDICATION iii

TABLE OF CONTENTS vii

FOREWORD ix

CHAPTER 1: Growing Though the Pain 1

CHAPTER 2: His Abuse, God's Vision 15

CHAPTER 3: Why Won't the Tears Go Away? 27

CHAPTER 4: Life on the Other Side of Violence 35

CHAPTER 5: Finding Peace Through This Journey 47

CHAPTER 6: God Was There All Along 57

CHAPTER 7: Survival Mode; Changed Mindset 69

CHAPTER 8: If I Only Knew 75

CHAPTER 9: No Longer on the Run 89

CHAPTER 10: Life Beyond the Shelters 95

CHAPTER 11: Triggers Will Come 101

CHAPTER 12: My Story Isn't Over 115

CHAPTER 13: A Woman No Longer Deceived 133

CHAPTER 14: Driven By Purpose 143

ABOUT THE AUTHOR 155

A-WAY-OUT MINISTRIES 157

Daisy Arness Marrs

FOREWORD

By
Tony McGee
Senior Pastor, Zion Hope Church

The bible speaks of various women who, although they had endured hardship in their lives, God was able to use them to bring glory to His name. Often, we think of Mary of Nazareth, who was the mother of Jesus. A woman persecuted for being pregnant outside of wedlock. Yet, God used her pain and hardship to bring about the birth of the Messiah, Jesus Christ.

We think of Ruth the Moabite who lost her husband and faced great tribulation without a protector. Yet, she had faith. She followed her mother-in-law to Israel, devoted herself to the Lord, and played a critical role in God's victory through her everyday faithfulness in the face of impossible circumstances. These women overcame their obstacles, kept their faith in God, and were used in extraordinary ways.

I believe that Daisy Arness Marrs is cut from the same cloth as these strong women of faith. Her book is a testimony to the power of God and how through faith, you can overcome obstacles, conquer your challenges and face your darkest fears.

Her book, *Woman to Woman, Domestic Violence a Wrong Turn in Life*, is unapologetically real. It also helps give hope to the hopeless and brings healing to those hurting. Daisy is a strong woman of faith, whom I have the pleasure of knowing for over a decade and serving as her pastor. I applaud her willingness to use her story to bring God glory and to help others along the way.

From a place of darkness and difficulty, Daisy has used her experiences and committed herself to being a force against domestic violence. She speaks for those who feel lost, forgotten, and lonely. I encourage you to read every word and consider every thought as she takes you on a personal journey that will encourage you and inspire you to rise up against the forces of evil and domestic violence.

- *Pastor Tony McGee*

CHAPTER 1: Growing Though the Pain

My childhood was somewhat short-lived. The abuse I saw caused me to grow up at a young age. Abuse will often take you in directions that you didn't know you would go and cause you to experience things you never knew you could endure. I have fond memories of the long country roads, playing in the red dirt, and making mud pies with my siblings and cousins. When we lived in the country, life was simple. I cannot tell you when the mistreatment began because it feels like it was always there, especially during the times when I was in the presence of my father. When I was a young girl, I was told my father did not accept me as his child simply because of the color of my skin. Although I did not understand why, at that time, I was treated differently than my siblings. I would not know the answer until much later in life, and that is when it all made sense to me.

I still remember how he treated me in comparison to my older sister who had a darker skin complexion than me. My mother told me I was a pretty baby, just as fat with no hair on my head. I even won a baby contest, and yes, I took first place. She told me when I was a baby, my complexion was so light I looked like I was white. For this reason, I experienced rejection early in life by the one person you would think would love me simply because I am his child, my father.

His reasoning confused me because my father's father was mixed. My grandfather was half white and half black, but he looked white. When I was a child, no one of black ancestry was called mixed. They were called mulattos, a term that carried over from the 1920s and was assigned to children born to one white and one black parent. While researching my paternal family's genealogy, I found a census record that listed my grandfather's race as mulatto. Although I did not know this as a child, I am still somewhat confused as to why my father treated me differently since one of his sisters had a light-skinned complexion the same as mine.

My father put the kind of fear in me that no child should have to endure at any age. That fear was further complicated by favoritism. My father openly favored my older sister over me. Later in life, my mother shared that my brother, who was born a couple of years later, shared the same skin tone as my older sister, which furthered my father's suspicion that I was not his child. My brother was stillborn, and my sister continued her reign as the favorite child. Then it happened! Two years after my brother's birth, my younger sister was born, and 'lo and behold' she was light skinned with fair complexion, too.

Although I was happy there was someone else who looked like me, it was too late for me to create a loving bond with my father an estranged relationship had already been established. As I got older, he tried developing a better relationship between us, but his effort never lasted for long. The favoritism he showed my older sister would always resurface.

My family is from Cadiz, Kentucky, one of those small towns where everyone is almost related to each other. My mother gave birth to me and my siblings with the assistance of midwives, in our grandmother's home. There were no hospitals in town, so I was born on my grandmother's couch. My mother said I almost hit the floor when I came into the world. I was a big baby, weighing in at over nine pounds. I can still hear the arguments my parents would have and remember how my mother's younger brother, FB Tyler, would step in to protect her.

Uncle B, as we lovingly called him, was like a father figure to us as we grew up, and he protected us in many ways. He was my refuge from my father and showed me the love I needed. My father decided to relocate the family to another state. All the family we knew and loved, including Uncle B, were left behind. I remember traveling for what seemed forever in a crowded truck with my family on dirt roads to the place we would call home. The rough roads made for difficult travel, but we would reach our destination without incident. My father relocated our family to Indianapolis, Indiana in search of new job opportunities.

As you can imagine, there is a huge difference between living in the country and moving to a big city. At first, I dearly missed running freely in our yard, feeding pigs in my grandparent's back yard, the red dirt roads, plucking the chickens, and cleaning fish with my grandmother. Ultimately, my siblings and I would spend our summer vacations in Cadiz with our grandmother and the rest of our family. These would be our most cherished memories. We were home again and realized how we missed everyone when we'd return.

When we first arrived in Indianapolis, we lived on the south of the city in Barrington. We moved into an apartment building that was much different than what we were used to back home in Cadiz. Our apartment had a bathroom with a shower and bathtub and running water. In Cadiz, we heated our homes with a coal-burning stove, had outhouses for toilets, and initially had no running water in our homes. This was something we were not used to, but we enjoyed it. We missed our family back home, and the freedom of country living in Kentucky. We also had to get used to the ceiling lights because in Cadiz we were accustomed to oil-burning lamps to light our house.

I remember the abuse from my father towards my mother and how fearful we were when the yelling and hitting would start. Once we moved away, Uncle B was not there to help us any longer. It seemed as if the yelling and fighting grew worse once we moved to Indianapolis. I remember the sound of a gunshot in which my mother was shot in the leg after knocking the gun away from her head. I did not know the extent of the abuse nor that night's events until many years later when the bullet was removed from her leg, and she shared her story with us. As a child, I did not have the capacity to connect what I saw and heard as domestic violence, because I did not know what the term meant.

I remember one day my mother did not come home. My siblings and I were left with our father in that apartment all alone. We did not see our mother in what seemed like a lifetime to three little girls under seven years old. We didn't know where she was, and we were very afraid. I remember waking up in the middle of the night to go to the bathroom, it was dark in the bedroom I shared with my siblings. Suddenly, my father appeared in the hallway out of nowhere with no clothes on and it frightened me. I was so frightened that I hid next to a dresser in our bedroom. With only a small faint light coming from the hallway, I saw him go back in the room he had just emerged from. I didn't know what had caused him to come out of his room, or if he had heard me moving around. Instead of going to the bathroom, I went back to bed. When my father opened his bedroom door, I saw my mother's friend lying in my parent's bed. That one incident taught me a lesson I would carry in my heart, trust no one around someone you love, especially those you call a friend. The significance was lost on me then, but as a teenager I shared that story with my mother.

I recall one day the police showed up at our apartment door and our mother was behind them. My siblings and I were so happy to see her but were afraid when we saw the police. We ran to her with the biggest smiles on our faces, we were so excited to see her. Yes, our mother had come to take my sisters and me out of the apartment where we lived with our father. We did not know that she had planned to leave him and had gone to find us another place to stay. I remember when our father found us after we left, and the fear we experienced when he tried to attack our mother. During the attack, a man came to help her. That was the last time I remember seeing my father for many years. After we left, I remember us missing him, but not the abuse he came with.

I recall growing up when I would try to get my father's attention any way I could. No matter how hard I tried to please him, I never received the attention I craved. Later we found out that he had moved to Cleveland, Ohio. He sent for my older sister to visit him, but not my younger sister and me. After a while, he eventually sent for all three of us.

My father remarried and I remember having a stepsister that I was jealous of.

The first time I saw his reaction towards her and how he treated her compared to how he treated me, I was angry. In my young and immature mind, I believed all the attention she received from our father belonged to me. I often wondered how he could accept someone else's children as if they were his own, but not one of his own children. I couldn't understand my feelings and I tried my best to put them away and enjoy being in his presence again. Although I did not understand it then, I came to realize that when someone remarries and children are involved, they must accept them as their own. This lesson would become meaningful later in my life. As time went on, my mother met men who were just as mean and abusive as our father.

I also experienced mental abuse at a very young age. It would shape how I viewed myself and who I would eventually attract in my own life. I became very shy and withdrawn. Although from the outside you could not tell, I tried my best to fit in. I didn't make friends as quickly as other kids, and I did my best not to be rejected by them. What does a toxic environment teach young girls? Do we live and learn by what we see? Is this what life is meant to be with men? Why are men so abusive? These questions and many others plagued my mind.

Eventually, as I got older, I began to understand the motivations behind those questions and that no one is supposed to be abused in any way. Learning, growing, living, and developing through the pain of any abuse takes years to understand, and it should not have played a role in my growth and development as a child. Similarly, growth and development for children should not be stunted because of abuse or witnessing domestic violence. I, like countless other children, should have been able to trust those who have been assigned as our caregivers.

Life with my siblings was great after my father was no longer in our lives. My mother took great care in protecting us. She worked hard and, as a single mother of three young girls, she did the best she could with what she had available. We were never hungry and were very well-groomed. I remember the little purses that matched our outfits and shoes, and my mother dressed my older sister and me like twins. I remember someone stealing our little purses while we were playing outside. We ran inside to tell our mom, but when we returned, they were gone. Regardless, for a while it was just us, and life was good.

The times when we were able to get to know one another without the presence of men were some of the best I can remember. There were some not-so-great moments too. I remember how scared we were the times when my mother would pass out on the floor. My mother sacrificed a lot for us, more than we knew at the time. We learned later in life that she was passing out because she would make sure we were fed even if she did not have enough for herself. She would have fainting spells because of being so weak.

As a single mother of three young girls with no support from our father, she struggled hard to pay the bills alone. But she managed it while keeping food on the table, and we were never without a roof over our heads. As a single working mother, she had to find a babysitter to watch us. There came a time when our mother taught us how to stay home alone, because of the abuse we received while in the care of some of the babysitters. My siblings and I were experiencing more abuse than any other kids we knew at our age. What is so astounding is that I never knew how abnormal it was to grow up this way, because it was our only reality.

I remember one babysitter who would steal the food my mother would send for us to eat. She would make us stay in one corner of the living room until our mother picked us up. Once our mother found out how we were being treated, it was the last time we stayed at a babysitter's house. That experience taught me that abuse can come in any form, by anybody, and at any time. My mother was barely twenty years old when she had to figure out how to be a mother. She had her first child at fifteen and she had me at sixteen. How do girls learn how to become women? At what age do we realize we are no longer girls? I would wonder if anyone knew the answers to these questions that were constantly on my mind.

As young girls, my siblings and I were taught not to answer the door or the phone, and our mother would come home on her break from work to check on us and bring us our dinner. We moved often growing up, but when my mother purchased her first home it was a major accomplishment for her. But neither the location in which we lived nor the successes my mother experienced professionally seemed to change the men that she attracted. They were mostly abusive to her. During the remainder of our childhood years and as teenagers, this was constant with my mother. Continuing to witness abuse made us think that this was somehow normal. As teenagers, we found ourselves protecting our mother from the abuse she constantly endured. There were times when we would jump in to help her escape when she was being attacked. We learned as young girls to take care of ourselves, and we continued doing so while our mother worked long and late hours to provide for us. I remember getting my first job and helping take care of my siblings. My youngest sibling was born during this time, and I enjoyed taking care of her and learning her personality. My sisters and I loved taking care of her. Working while in school became part of my norm.

My older sister and I enjoyed running track in grade school. One day while in our eighth-grade gym class, we were outside, and a boy was crossing the courtyard where our gym class was running track. My oldest sister was good at running and seemed to outrun everyone out there. The boy had stopped and asked a friend of mine if she knew who I was. I didn't see him again until I went to high school. I was dating someone else at the time when I saw him again. That is when he started to aggressively pursue me. Although I was not interested in him, he wouldn't let up until I eventually gave in. Because of the abuse I witnessed in my home life, I should have seen this as a sign.

Looking back, it was not as if I took an interest in him. It was his persistence in getting what he wanted that I should have seen as a red flag. He did not respect my space or my wishes. Did I feel pressured into a relationship with him? Yes. I was fifteen years old and heading into my sophomore year of high school and he was a senior. I had never learned the skills on how to prevent situations like this from occurring. Why are there no classes to teach young girls how to protect themselves as they mature?

I remember the first time he hit me. My friend and I were at a house party over the weekend when he showed up. I was so ashamed of what happened that the next morning I called my friend who went to the party with me and asked her not to tell anybody what happened. What I failed to realize at the time, was that many people from school had seen it as well. I remember the whispers when I returned to school on Monday about the incident. In the beginning, without realizing it, I started protecting him and making excuses for his action. Keep in mind that I was the one that was abused, but I didn't worry about myself even though I was the one injured. Why is this acceptable? Why do we ignore our own feelings for the need to protect our abuser? Even as these questions inundated me, I couldn't behave in any other way. My upbringing had conditioned me to believe this behavior was acceptable and normal. What I know today is that this behavior is never okay! Never!

Unintentionally, I had given him permission to control me by using physical force for the remainder of our relationship. Please pay attention to this! Do what I was unable to do for myself; know your worth and fight for it. For me, this was the time when red flags should have gone up and forced me to realize what was happening. If I am being honest, there were red flags even before he hit me the first time. I tried to break things off with him, but he wouldn't leave me alone. My mother would even try to keep me from seeing him, but he would always find his way back, and I would eventually step back in the relationship. I remember wondering if there are things that an abuser sees in a girl's vulnerability that makes them think they can be controlling over them.

As I mentioned previously, my mother attempted to end our relationship, however, the years of witnessing her abuse set me up as the perfect victim to this perpetrator of my own. He became someone who wanted ALL my attention. If I was not at school or work, he was with me. He controlled my time. This caused me to miss a lot of my high school functions and activities. My freshman year was great! I loved participating in talent shows, running track, and singing in the choir. When I was a senior, I joined the girl's football team and attended the senior prom. Of course, he was there too.

I did not have many friends, but I had a best friend who seemed to have the same issues I did, though we did not share everything with each other. I am sure the shame we both experienced kept us from sharing what was going on in our relationships. Even though I couldn't protect myself, I found myself being very protective of my siblings. I would help my mother by making sure they had lunch money for school, and I even filled out the documentation they needed to attend. As a teenager I took on responsibilities as a guardian, and became my sisters' go-to person. As I reflect on my high school years, I see how much I missed that my friends participated in. While I saw my friends graduate high school and go off to college, I worked to help support my siblings and care for our home.

What was college? Not a subject we talked about in our home. After all, my mother was married with children at an early age and ended up dropping out of school to raise us. She taught me several very important life lessons without knowing it. One such lesson was that you can only teach what you know! Coming straight from the south, my parents' family did not attend college or complete high school. They were focused on trying to make it in the world as best they could.

I always had dreams of becoming a nurse, and I remember my siblings and I would play doctor and nurse when we were young girls. One day I decided I was going to attend nursing school and follow my dream. But life intervened, and it was a long while before I would receive my nursing license. The struggles with being abused, trying to hide it, working, and going to school were difficult. You see, no one knew I was being abused while attending nursing school, or why I was so distracted. The makeup would cover the bruises, and the long hair over my face prevented people from seeing my puffy eyes from the tears I cried at night.

As I think back on the things I went through just to live my dream of being a nurse, they were innumerable and disheartening. My abuser tore up my books, causing me to fail tests and experience many nights with tears streaming down my face. They were all attempts to destroy my dream of becoming a nurse. As I failed my first attempt at nursing school, I saw my dream fall by the wayside. I remember him laughing and teasing because he thought he'd succeeded in ripping my dream away from me. Once again, I would watch students walk into their vocations while my heart ached as I yearned to walk into mine.

The guilt and shame stayed with me a long time after that. I lacked self-confidence and the willingness to go and talk to my instructors about what I was going through. More importantly, if they saw the evidence of my abuse, why did they not intervene when they saw the fluctuations in my attitude and moods? There were days I would be cheerful and other days I would be withdrawn and depressed. Why was no one paying attention when my grades went from A's to failures, missing multiple days of class or missing assignments? I would sometimes wonder if anyone could help me. Could their interference have been the end of the abuse? It took me a long time to grasp the significance of what I was asking, and to understand the implications in my life. I am sure it is the same for others. I challenge you not to be afraid to reach out to someone you trust. Give them the opportunity to help you! Do not do what I did and stay in that relationship.

I stayed long after I had lost my identity, destroyed what little self-esteem I had and unintentionally introduced my daughter to a lifestyle that no child should have to witness. I was a daughter walking in her mother's footsteps of abuse and did not realize it. Is anyone willing to put themselves out there to help someone that seems to have changed both mentally and physically? As teachers, mentors, leaders, and interested bystanders, how will you pay attention to the signs of abuse you see? Will you get involved? As an employer, how will you assist an employee who shows signs of being abused in their actions, behaviors, or appearance? As a community, are we willing to pay close enough attention to see when someone has become withdrawn? Are we willing to learn the signs, symptoms, and the face of abuse to become a resource for them?

Reflection: Although I was rejected at an early age by my father, I always had my Heavenly Father who loves me. We often hear boys need their fathers to show them how to be men, but young girls need them as well to show them how to be loved, respected, and treated by men.

"I will be a Father to you, and you will be my sons and daughters, says the Lord Almighty."

2 Corinthians 6:18, NIV

CHAPTER 2: His Abuse, God's Vision

I was twenty-three years old and ready to purchase my first home. We were finally done with apartment living and purchased what I thought was a wonderful home. We now had a place where our daughter could play safely outside. I searched for a daycare and found one around the corner from our home. I was very particular about who cared for my daughter, as I had already lost my son. I gave birth to my first child at the age of nineteen, and he passed away in my arms. That experience caused me to be very protective of my daughter. I remember clearly as my son was struggling in the hospital and asking the Lord to take him back with Him instead of asking Him to heal him. I could not take his suffering anymore, and God called my son home. Be careful what you pray for because you just might get it.

I did not know it then, but our prayers are heard. And whatever we ask for, we must be prepared to receive. After losing my son, my beloved Uncle B, my father figure, made sure he was there for me. I did not hear from my biological father at that time, but my best friend Sheila showed up to support me. I became fastidious about my daughter's care as both of my children were born prematurely. The ladies at the daycare became attached to my daughter very quickly, and they took good care of her, so I didn't have to worry.

I remember when we received the call that my father had passed away. It was 1994, and I found myself sitting on my bedroom floor crying hard, not understanding why he never apologized to me. I would never have the opportunity to talk to my father about how he made me feel growing up, or how he impacted my life going forward. How do you forgive someone who never asked for forgiveness?

In my own way, I have offered emotional forgiveness to my biological father for completely selfish reasons. I needed to move on with the business of living and learn how to offer myself the love and acceptance I always craved from him.

My new home was just what was needed at the time, so I thought. I was extremely excited about decorating and buying new furniture. You know how it feels when you have accomplished one of your goals in life, well this was another one of mine. My daughter's room looked outside to the backyard, and she seemed to enjoy it. She was able to see her swing set out her window, as she enjoyed playing at the park, and now can enjoy the outdoors in her own backyard. It was exciting to show family and friends our new home.

We had wonderful neighbors, and everything seemed like it would be okay because I found a place to raise my daughter safely. She was able to meet new friends and enjoy everything that children would enjoy in a house instead of apartment living. We were able to establish relationships with our neighbors that would be beneficial to our safety as new homeowners in the neighborhood.

Eventually, darkness would enter our new home. We think that if we do positive things that it will change our circumstances, but it will not. Drugs and abuse continued to dominate the world of my home. Life as I knew it had changed drastically, and in terms of abuse, it had gotten worse. The red flags were always there, even at the beginning of the relationship. They would show up now and again to let me look at them in the eye, but I had no idea what they were or why they were there. What appeared to be normal for me would have been devastation for someone else.

I had to find a way out of the abuse to protect my daughter and save my life. I knew it was time to take drastic measures. Figuring out how to do it was hard. What was it I was trying to do? Why didn't I just leave well enough alone? Will it even make a difference? Maybe I should just stay and hope things will improve? Once again, questions showed up without providing me with a light at the end of the darkness. I had no idea what to do or where to start! I did know that I had to do for my daughter what my mother was brave enough to do for me. It wasn't until that moment when I realized that what she had done was brave and courageous. My mother found the courage to be brave at a time when everything around her was hopeless. She faced that hopelessness and found the strength to change our circumstances for the better. Where was I to begin? There were no written instructions on how to get away from an abuser.

Oftentimes images of domestic violence were shown on television of perpetrators killing their victims either because they wanted to leave them, tried to leave them, or after they had left and was found by them. I remember thinking that someone else is dealing with this too! I did not hear people talking about it though. I was beginning to realize that this couldn't be my life any longer. However, what I saw on television instilled fear in me, and that is why I stayed as long as I did. The fear that had attached itself to me was more convincing and more unknowable than continuing to live with the abuse.

I know some people wonder why it is so hard to leave. A significant part has to do with the psychological and emotional abuse the victim endures, and the knowledge of what the abuser is capable of that keeps the victim tied to their abuser. I shared earlier that I tried to end our relationship, but I kept getting pulled back into it. This is also true for other victims as well. They realize the relationship is unhealthy and desire to exit it, but every time they try to leave, they get pulled right back in. They go back without understanding that the cycle of abuse is what their abuser uses to control them.

My home had become a prison, but I still had a dream of becoming a nurse, and I was not going to give that up. To support my family, I went to school and received my Cosmetology license. It was a means to an end, but it wasn't my dream. Although I enjoyed doing hair, something was still missing in my life. Eventually, I signed up again for nursing school. It was hard and the nights were long, but I loved it. Studying was a hard task because I was working, taking care of my daughter, and financially providing for our home as the sole provider. I had figured out a unique way of studying this time, even if the books got torn up. He was not going to keep me from fulfilling my dream any longer.

I eventually got up the nerve to hire a lawyer, file for a legal separation, and get a restraining order against him. Was I afraid? Of course, I was terrified. Fear of the unknown can take you to a place of torment. I remember it taking a while to sign the papers because I was petrified. When I signed the papers, it would all become real. I was headed for the fight of my life. Was I prepared for it? Absolutely not! I remember the day my attorney told me he filed the papers with the courts, and a court date would eventually be given. The panic and fear that struck me were indescribable! I realized I had made a major decision on my own that would permanently impact my life going forward.

I remember thinking, what was I supposed to do when he was served with the papers? How can I protect my child if something were to happen to me? What would happen to her? The waiting period was excruciating. Each day was more terrifying than the day before. I reasoned that I would be safe from losing my life because I hadn't filed for divorce. I thought I made a sound decision to protect myself and my child. One step at a time is how I viewed it. A knife in my back was my reward for filing for a legal separation.

A few days after the papers were filed, I was asleep in my bed, my daughter was in her bedroom sleeping, and I was awakened suddenly when I felt someone straddling my back. As I looked back while attempting to turn over, I saw a glint of steel and realized I was staring at a knife in the hand of my now ex-husband. I was slightly disoriented from being unexpectedly awoken. It took me a while to realize that what had awoken me was him stabbing me in my back. While attempting to turn over with his body on top of me, I began to beg for my life. The look in his eyes horrified me, and it was an image that would haunt me for a very long time. I begged and begged until he finally got off me. It was almost as if he held the knife tighter still, if that was even possible. I was fully awake when I finally realized that he planned on killing me that night.

As I tried to get up, I realized I was lying in a bed full of blood and that I could not stretch out my right leg. With tears streaming down my face, and fear in my heart, I knew something was very wrong. It was at that moment that I realized he had just stabbed me in my back. Standing there and begging for my life until he finally put his arm down from the position to stab me again, I asked for him to call an ambulance for me. As I limped through the house, I found myself trying to get away from him while begging him for help. He would not let me out of his sight and followed me wherever I went.

I stayed as calm as I could to try to not worsen the situation or frighten my daughter. Even though my daughter stayed sleeping in her room, I was afraid for her safety. She told me much later in life, during one of our discussions, that she had been asleep until awakened by my mother. Once out of bed, she tried to come into the room where I was, but my mother stopped her from entering.

He finally agreed to call my mother only if I would agree to say I fell against the floor model television in my bedroom. Of course, at this point I would agree to anything. When my mother arrived and noticed that I was injured she called 911 for an ambulance not realizing what had happened. She saw the blood and saw that I was injured and could barely walk. Just before my mother arrived, he opened the back door, took the knife he had held in his hand, and threw it as far as he could. When the fire department and ambulance arrived, he told the first responders how my injury had occurred. His version of the events, not the truth.

I do not think either the fire department personnel or the ambulance attendants believed his story, but it was all they had to go on at the time. Once I was in the ambulance, they asked me what really happened, and I informed them that I was stabbed in the back by my ex-husband. On the way to the hospital, the ambulance drivers changed the code, put on their lights and sirens, and called the police and the emergency room doctors. The police met us at the hospital, but by that time I had no idea where my ex-husband had gone. My mother and other family members arrived at the hospital and learned what had happened to me. A sense of calm had come over me while heading to the hospital, and I cannot explain why. I am not sure if it was because I was no longer in his presence, or if for the first time since meeting him I felt safe and protected. As I think back on that night, I realize the feeling came over me when the first responders rescued me from the death sentence my ex-husband had spoken over my life.

Once in the hospital emergency room, the physician examined and cleaned the wound on my upper back. Afterward, they were going to release me into my mother's care, but I told them something else was wrong because I could not extend my right leg. The conversation surprised me because the doctors never asked me if I had any other symptoms related to the stab wound. The doctors then decided to admit me for further evaluation and ordered an MRI of my back early the next morning.

The next morning my younger sister Crystal was visiting me when a group of doctors came into my hospital room. They wanted to share with me the results of the MRI scan and asked if it was okay to share the information while my sister was present. With my sister by my side, they informed me that the knife had indeed penetrated my spine and it was the cause of me not being able to extend my leg. Tears started rolling down both me and my sister's face. They also shared that the infection control physicians would be taking over because the knife had penetrated a sterile area and could cause Bacterial Meningitis.

Intravenous antibiotics were started immediately. However, the infection had already started to infect my body. The main symptom I felt was a headache that was very painful, much worse than a migraine headache. I could not keep my eyes open due to photosensitivity. Since it would be painful for the lights to have contact with my eyes, I sat in my dark hospital room for a couple of days while receiving antibiotic therapy. Bacterial Meningitis was trying to take hold of my body while traveling to my brain. Had I not demanded to be checked by the emergency room doctors further, I would not be here to share my story with you.

I walked with a limp for over a year from the damage caused when my ex-husband stabbed me in the back. If I walked at a normal or fast pace, the limp was noticeable. In order to keep people from noticing the limp, I would walk very slowly. And I mean *very* slowly. I remember while staying at my mother's house after being released from the hospital, I tried to walk to get rid of the limp, to no avail. I would get up and try to walk every day, back and forth across the floor. But it would not go anywhere. Instead of being grateful for being alive, at the time I was angry about the limp and would often cry about it when alone.

After months of physical therapy, the limp diminished over time. Though I do have a slight limp to this day. There are other residual effects from the stab wound to my spine that will affect my right lower limb forever. The injury to my spine made me more compassionate towards people diagnosed with any form of paralysis. I understood firsthand how it feels when you lose the function of and no longer have control over a part of your body. Like so many other women, I incorrectly believed I would somehow be protected because I did not file for divorce. He knew that when I filed for the separation it was my way of saying I had enough.

This did not stop him from attempting to take my life again. It was just the beginning of the journey he and I would take. I could not believe it! What I saw on the television was happening to me. I remember taking my daughter to visit her paternal grandmother, per her request, and it was a huge mistake on my part. Of all the mistakes I have made in my life, this one was right up there at the top of the list. When his mother realized what he was planning to do, she tried to remove the knife out of his hand when he attempted to stab me. Yep, he tried it again. Yes, I left my daughter there and that was such a huge mistake because he was there when I returned to pick her up. This experience taught me to not trust my ex-husband's side of the family because they were also being manipulated either by knowing or not knowing what his intentions were regarding me. His mother prevented me from using her phone to call 911 but allowed me to call my mother. A mother will try to protect their child in any way possible. Knowing that, I am still grateful for her intervening and fighting to take the knife out of his hand that day.

My mother showed up quickly and took me and my daughter out of that dangerous situation. I finally got up the nerve to file for a divorce, but to my detriment I continued living in the house instead of moving. He broke into the house and this time he began choking me. Once again, I found myself fighting for my life. Suddenly, there was a loud banging at my front door. The attack stopped as he went to answer the front door. It was the police. My daughter had gotten out of her bed and ran downstairs and called 911 without either of us knowing it. That was the first and last time he was ever placed in handcuffs and taken to jail.

After filing for a restraining order and expecting the police to protect me and my daughter, I learned that restraining orders or protective orders are not worth the paper they are written on. They do not protect the victims as they should. There is story after story of women who have filed a restraining or protective order and they were not enforced by the police, which leaves the victim to fend for themself. As a result, many lives are lost to domestic violence even when the orders are in place. Procedures need to change as to how the court system keeps track of the individuals who violate a protective order.

My life was saved that night because of the actions of my brave 6-year-old daughter. It was much later in life when my daughter shared with me that her father had noticed her in the hallway that night not realizing she had just come from downstairs calling the police and it scared her. However, it did not stop him from attacking me that night. That was the last time he would have an opportunity to attack me in the house. I decided right then and there that it was time to pack up and move. My daughter and I were able to safely and successfully relocate after all the trauma we experienced in that house.

God had a purpose and a vision already predestined for my life. He kept me amid the storm. Zephaniah 3:17(NIV) says, *"The Lord your God is in your midst, a mighty one who will save; He will rejoice over you with gladness; He will quiet you by His love; He will exult over you with loud singing."* Although my earthly father was never there for me, my heavenly Father was always there, watching, protecting, and wiping away the tears I shed and the ones I hid in my heart. God kept me anchored through the storm of abuse, although going through it caused me to experience a lot of trauma. I am so very thankful that I came out of it victoriously. Yes, my dream of becoming a nurse was eventually obtained and my ex-husband was never able to destroy God's vision for my life in becoming a nurse. What he did, without realizing it, was strengthen my resolve, and I began living my purpose. The end of our relationship was the beginning of me living my life, rather than merely existing.

Reflection: Even through the storms of life, God's vision for us is greater. Do not ever give up on your dreams, no matter how hard it is for you to reach them. Although there will be obstacles in your way at times, your will to accomplish what is yours should be even greater.

"Write the vision; make it plain on tablets, so he may run who reads it."

Habakkuk 2:2 –ESV

CHAPTER 3: Why Won't the Tears Go Away?

As a survivor of domestic violence, there are many questions that have kept my heart and mind actively trying to find an answer. Why do women and children continue to be killed in domestic disturbances the same way they were fifteen, twenty, and even thirty years ago? Why are restraining orders and protective orders ineffective? Is there another process that can be used to protect women from the start? Who will step up to the plate and help protect victims? Why is our pain still so strong and why does it still hurt so much? Why do we feel unprotected and fearful of dying at the hands of the man we went to the law to get away from so many times before? Why do we still dream of this man taking our lives? These questions remain today as to why the law is not protecting victims of domestic violence as it should. Lastly, why do we still feel like victims? Is domestic violence now normalized as victims stay in fear? Our children are fearful and somehow seem to follow in our footsteps, at least some do. We must break the generational curses that seem to be normalizing domestic violence.

Women and children are still dying from these violent crimes. Anger, fear, and insecurity are strong in the minds of their victims, especially for those who feel their abusers are controlling their thoughts, emotions, and lives. Who will help us stop the tears? There are men who say they are reformed batterers and want to help other men control their anger toward their female counterparts. But who will step in to teach these women how to lead normal lives? If those who have been abused do not survive, who will keep their memories alive? These former abusers all seem to go on to lead normal lives. As for the victims, they do not know what normal is! Victims often experience confusion and frustration, especially with laws that will not take away the rights of their abusers.

While victims continue to die and live in fear, men continue to make the laws meant to protect them. Then why do women follow the letter of the law, only to lose their precious lives? Why don't they leave and trust the law to protect them? Well, as I shared earlier, statistics show that once a woman seeks assistance from the police and attempts to leave their abuser, is the point when their life becomes expendable. They are in even more danger than before of losing their life. I experienced this firsthand. I ignorantly believed that by filing for a separation instead of a divorce, I was saving my life.

When speaking about the issues that women, children, and some men face, it appears to be a very lonely place. No one seems to be listening and there is no understanding as to why. Most of society thinks that this may be an individual choice because people stay in the relationship. It often takes time to understand that a relationship is unhealthy because after all violence is so prevalent today. It is unthinkable to others looking in from the outside as to why one will not leave an abusive relationship. However, more often than not, compassion is needed instead of judgment because it is then and only then that the cycle of abuse can be recognized, and effective systems put in place to eradicate domestic violence.

Without realizing it many victims have accepted fear as a trusted companion because they have become familiar with its presence in their life. The victims understand, and to a certain extent, they accept the situation they find themselves in because of the dire circumstances surrounding them leaving. Why should a victim be expected to leave when they have heard on many occasions about a victim who attempted to leave or have left but did not survive their next encounter with their abuser? This is their reality and for many victims, including myself, they determine it is better to keep themselves in the situation and live quietly. The sad thing is, that mindset leads to us struggling to be safe while struggling to stay alive.

All victims want a way out! They are consistently hoping someone will understand and help them develop an escape plan that does not lead to them losing their life. In the same way women with low self-esteem can be in a room full of people and feel lonely, a victim of domestic abuse can be in a room full of people and feel invisible. No one is seeing them or recognizing how unhappy they are. They want to fit in with the crowd but cannot because they are in survival mode. Happiness is short-lived outside their homes and quickly turns to sadness once they re-enter their home and their place of darkness. Victims do not realize that happiness surrounds them outside their place of darkness because their minds cannot see past their present circumstances. Every moment alive is seen as a place of refuge for the time being because they can at least take a deep breath. The battlefields on their bodies reveal that their scars are reminders of how they must live in fear, and so they stay. It is as if they are locked in a house of mirrors with only the ability to see and experience the loneliness, while simultaneously fearing the unknown.

Still, questions arise as to why the tears will not go away? Why won't they stop? We consistently hear about domestic violence statistics and the people who live in violent situations, but we do not hear of their life on the other side of it. We do not hear how a victim is to survive once they leave the darkness. Nightly visions appear, and distant cries are heard while the darkness of the night creeps in. These are the times when I realized there was nowhere to run or hide. I felt as if I was being held captive in my own fear. Whether in the newspaper or on the news, we are always hearing about the ones who did not survive. Questions come to mind that is demanding an answer, "who is protecting us? Is it worth the risk?"

I think back to my mother and the courage she found to take us out of the abusive household we were born into. I know the stories, I heard the reports, and I was one that experienced the fear. However, the desire to have a better life was stronger than the fear I had been living with. Anything is better than where I was back then! I had finally come to the realization that no one was coming to save us. I thought I had to find the courage to save myself and my daughter! Everyone who experiences that type of abuse must take up the courage to make that a reality.

Amid the dark times, many questions have come about as to why these issues remain in our society. Many people live in darkness, not only in the home but also in their mind. They are forever running to escape the fear. There are several symptoms wrapped up in the mind that finds its way into the body, so that the mind no longer listens to the victim's wishes. The same body that longs to be free from the disasters it has been ravaged by. A body that has become so unfamiliar and repulsive, you cannot even look at her in the mirror without becoming physically ill. A body that is caught in a cycle of violence and is unable to find itself because it has become so unfamiliar. A body that is paralyzed by the uncertainty of its survival. As the courage begins to build and the fearlessness begins to seep into every being of you, then you begin to understand that it is a body that was predestined to be free.

As people go about living their lives, many do not realize that a victim of domestic violence is trying to survive on the diminishing reserves of their strength. As they live through the emotional, mental, and physical abuse, they find themselves caught up in the darkness of pain and grief. They wonder why these events continue to happen. I kept seeing the happiness I desired but it was just outside of my reach. I could not grab hold of it, and I began telling myself it did not belong to me anyway. So, why am I trying to have it? As my mind began to play tricks on me, I would imagine the happiness I desired in my life. It was only a glimpse. I realize it was not my life, but someone else's. The more I thought about it, the more I wanted it. The idea or concept of happiness seemed to capture my thoughts, especially during those times when I felt all alone in a world where I had no desire to be.

I heard a small voice telling me it is mine for the taking. I told myself, that cannot be. Nothing good, other than my children, had ever happened in my life since I met him. I found myself thinking about the happiness that small voice said I could have. Is it meant to be mine? I remember hearing in Church that happiness was sent from heaven just for me. Was God speaking to me? Was He trying to get my attention? Was He attempting to redirect my thoughts to stop me from contemplating my existence as it relates to the madness that had entered my world?

Can you see the fear on the faces of a child caught in the cycle of abuse? How can anyone allow this to continue or blame it on the victim because of something they must have done? As I consider the ramifications of those questions, the shadows of the life I had always wanted continued to pass me by. I remember struggling trying to grab hold of it. Every time I thought I had it, I realized it was just outside of my reach. It had gotten more and more frustrating as I tried to make it become a part of my reality to enjoy the freedoms it offered. As the fear again appeared, it caused me to tremble when I tried to find my destiny and reach out beyond myself. Fear was all-consuming, and I stopped immediately as it once again grabbed hold of me. The shadows were pulling me deeper into a place of darkness where I could no longer see the shadows of happiness that were waiting on me. Will the darkness consume me? Will I die while I am in the darkness never able to see the light of happiness? So much of the darkness had control of my mind, and I found it was hard to shake at times.

Being lost in time and space, you try to see through the darkness of your existence when suddenly a thought appears, as if to say, "if only for a while outside the doors of fear can I let a smile creep in?" There's that small voice again assuring us that we will be ok. Time has become something no longer valuable because the darkness lasted so long and invaded every second of your life. You hear the sounds on the clock as it slowly ticks while identifying each second, minute, and hour as its hand creeps around the circle of its face. You realize while mesmerized by its movement that only seconds have passed. You then pray for light to overshadow the darkness that has found its way into your existence as time finally seems to come to a standstill.

Tears flow constantly as frustration finds itself resting upon you as if to force you to go in a different direction. A direction that would bring about change. The darkness stands as a constant reminder of the shadows in your life. You find yourself burying your thoughts into every hidden painful crevice of your being. A being that only exists because your abuser allowed it, and you had to beg for it. A being that is destined to be free from the torment of the mind and the scars that have taken up residence on your body. You have cried so many tears that you find yourself hoping that your tears would be tears of joy. You find yourself deep in the caves of darkness pursuing a way out. You somehow find yourself free in the caves of your lonely mind that is tormented to the depths of your soul.

You run deeper into the safe caves created in your mind and you realize you are only hanging on by a thread. The thread of light that is being destroyed by the loneliness of your thoughts. Thoughts in a mind that is seeking to devour your reality, and that are striving to find the hand of someone that will love the true you, the very nature and essence of who God says you are. You are longing to survive the torment of your mind and your body. Just when you think you may survive, your mind seems to be caught in a closed box. A box that just doesn't even exist anymore. A box that has been forgotten. A box that desires to be found. A box that seeks justice. A box that has kept the memories of the past and seeks the promise of a future. A box that yearns desperately to be noticed, taken to a safe place, and loved unconditionally. Then the realization hits like a ton of bricks, you are nothing more than a box!

You find yourself housed in torment and being destroyed from within. All while searching for peace—the peace that has escaped you for so long. A peace that must survive for you to survive. A peace that fills your contentment with the light of love. When that peace is received then the shadows of the darkness will fade into a place of redemption, release, and forgiveness. The redemption, release, and forgiveness have been waiting for you all along. They have been standing in the shadows of the darkness waiting for you to find your way out.

You must find a way out of the despair from living in a situation that has altered your life and your very being. You must find a way out of the situation that has turned your world upside down. A way out of what has become as dangerous as the devil's den. A way out of what once was and what feels like an eternity. You finally begin communicating with that small still voice and you ask Him to show you the way out. As He guides your footsteps and you become confident it is your way out, you then find yourself walking into a life on the other side of the emotional, mental, and physical abuse that you have continuously longed for. *You are now free!*

Reflection: There will be many times when you feel discouraged even though you know you have given your all. Continuously keep your mind focused on moving forward instead of what is causing you pain. It will eventually help to stop the tears.

"He will wipe every tear from their eyes."

Revelation 21:4 NIV

CHAPTER 4: Life on the Other Side of Violence

L ife on the other side of violence seems so far away for someone that experiences it. I often found myself thinking about why I did not feel loved. Ultimately, once I realized who I was in Christ he revealed his love for me because he is the very essence of love. Talking to God gave me a revelation about life and how I should be treated. I had to realize that we as women should have more power over our bodies and minds than men give us credit for. If we don't seek to learn about the men we come in contact with then all of their history comes with them good or bad. It is okay to do your research. After all, we would research a car before we purchased it to make sure of its value. It must be just as important to research someone that you decide to let into your life. Especially when we decide to give ourselves to them intimately.

I am no longer intimidated by men that try to dominate me either by words or actions. I will no longer live in the shadows of another person or be pushed aside as if I don't matter. Shadows are dark and get stepped on and I have the right to be seen. I no longer will give anyone that much power over me. Did you know that giving up your power also gives up control of who you are? Think about it, once you get into a relationship it is no longer about just you. It is imperative to seek and find out first. Now, I am quick to cut it off at the beginning. After all, I will not be intimidated or belittled in any way because I am a woman with a mind of her own. As women, we deserve to be respected, but we must respect ourselves first. We were uniquely made for a reason, not by accident, and not to be mistreated.

One day my sister-friends and I decided to purchase a book called *The Women of the Bible for Women of Color*. A particular woman in this book named Dinah caught my attention when reading it. This chapter I read spoke of Dinah being an abused woman. She was raped and needed someone to help her, but her father was silent. Men are often silent when it comes to abuse of women, and this is no longer acceptable. It brought back remembrance of how my father treated me because he was silent towards me in many ways. He did not protect me. In addition, what stood out in the chapter about Dinah was this statement, "They declared that a violation of one woman is an affront to the entire community." (Lockyer, 35) What a powerful statement. As women, we should speak loudly about the assault on women all over the world, and not let a single one remain unheard.

Domestic violence against one woman permits for it to continue if we are silent. I have chosen to live freely on the other side of the violence that held me captive for too long. You too can live this way. There are too many women in the bible that demonstrate strength, and they walked with Jesus. Jesus did not allow persecution of women. The book of John speaks about a woman caught in adultery. In the book of John 8:7 (NIV) Jesus says, *"Let any one of you who is without sin be the first to throw a stone at her."* Jesus stopped men from harming her, regardless of her sin. Us women have more power than we give ourselves credit for. I also know that our bodies are temples, and they should be treated as such.

Seeking God's voice became something that I strived for daily, and needed to hear to obtain peace. I had to sit still in my quiet space to hear His voice. I had questions to ask, and He loves for us to have personal conversations with him. Although my profession was in nursing, I needed to know who I was to become as a child of God. Keeping out the noise of the world can be difficult at times, but if we are quiet enough, we will hear Him. A survivor of domestic violence was not who I was supposed to become. I had indeed conquered death, so I am a conqueror. I needed God to help direct my path towards my future. I also had to learn about life on the other side of what could be, away from pain, torment, and darkness.

I was indeed searching for myself. The self that has permitted me to survive. With this knowledge, I had to learn how to establish a personal relationship with God. He became my trusted friend. John 15:13 (KJV) says *"Greater love hath no man than this, that a man lay down his life for his friends."* This verse gave me chills as I realized that God called me a friend and gave his own life for me. I had been given the grace to be free. I thought wow, what a great revelation. God has indeed given me the right to choose the life that will conquer all. I found myself looking through the mirror of my past, seeing straight through to my future. I began finding it was okay to release the memories of the past and grasp the present moment as if it were my last. I found myself hungry for life on the other side of violence that my daughter and I had experienced. It was very dark and lonely living there. I had learned how to lead in such a way that my past would not dictate my future and I loved living in the light that God provides.

My life has consisted of past failures from a relationship that I thought would last a lifetime. Even though I thought this, I knew it was not true. I also thought, there is no way that someone can continue living in a life of abuse and feel that God has placed them there. I had already been predestined for freedom, so how could an abusive relationship define me? God created me to be a free-being, not framed within an image that man had made for me. Therefore, I had broken the chains that had kept me imprisoned for so long. Broken people often seek patterns of familiarity. So, to break away from this pattern, I began to learn the love of God and how he gives love to others, and the chains no longer had power over me.

No matter my sins, He still loved me, and through confession of my sins, He forgave me. How can I look for this type of love and find it elsewhere? After all, the past is all I knew. I had to renew my mind by allowing my heart and mind to heal. For so many years I was broken, shattered, and isolated. Although I had been freed from the monster of the past, healing still had to take place. Once on the other side of it, I became aware of the freedoms that were taken from me, and that made me feel the curse of despair and injustice. I was furious at myself at times. Who was I outside of the person that held me captive so to speak?

There was so much of my life I could not get back, but there was so much more ahead that I was ready to go after. Learning that I was beautifully and wonderfully made by my Creator as scripture says, made me view my physical body differently. It gave me new insight into my human form. Psalm 139:14 says, *"My creator gave me a new insight about myself."* I began to fix my crown and wear it boldly for my light to shine. Ultimately, God showed me that I am a queen and only someone worthy to be sitting at the table of the King will be able to shift my crown. God's word tells us that we can be free from the guilt and shame that told us the lies. I was already free in spirit, it was only the physical body that was held captive.

I was freed from the monster that kept me under a tight rope. Sometimes you may find yourself pulling at the rope, only to find yourself falling to rock bottom. I pulled myself up to an area of winning once I stopped worrying about fitting in. No longer was I going to put myself last, I thought. I am more than enough. I am a child of God and have been saved from death.

As we know, being a woman brings about a lot of emotions. Releasing and forgiving myself took a while. First, I had to learn to forgive myself for allowing someone to abuse me for so long. I also had to forgive myself for not recognizing what it was. Then I had to forgive the court system for not protecting me and my daughter. When I paid for an attorney which I could not afford, we were still not protected. I did everything right according to the law, but almost lost my life instead. Indeed, I stopped beating myself up with words and in doing so I was building up my self-esteem. But I was still upset with the court system in how restraining orders are not protecting us.

With forgiveness came healing, and freedom from the mental hold that abuse had on my mind. I was in a dark place for a long time without knowing it. Don't let yourself get caught up like this because you could find yourself having suicidal tendencies. You *must* reject those thoughts. That was the longest part of the journey. Secondly, I had to be honest with myself. I had to admit to myself that I did not allow it to happen. It was simply all I knew from what I had seen growing up. It was there from the start, because my father was the contributing factor. Finally, I became aware that I mustn't pour myself into someone that wasn't deserving of the love that I had to give. I was no longer that person. My happiness will not be given to someone undeserving of that gift. What does this mean? I will not give my happiness to a person who wasn't designed for the gift God gave me. After all, so much time had been wasted from abuse that I did not know what happiness was or even felt like. After I figured it out, I protected it at all costs. I am now so full of gratitude in knowing who I am that my potential is beyond measure.

Toxic relationships of any kind will steal the joy that is God-given. So, stay completely clear from them. I've learned that I must not feel guilt for someone else's wrongdoing. I did this for so long. Therefore, I applaud myself for the distance that I put between them and me. Life on the other side of violence meant I had to stop attempting to change the people around me, but I had to change myself. Changing myself required a lot of studying the word of God. Figuring out who I was going to become was a major task because of the years of not knowing. Who was I outside of the person that had held me captive? I eventually learned that as seasons change, so do the people that come into your life. Some are only meant to be there for a season. As seasons of life change, so do we, or at least we should.

It took me a while to accept and understand that many people will bring chaos into your life. They also enjoy doing so. I'm sure you can think of some just by reading this. They could show up at any time, and may not make it known at the beginning, but it doesn't take long to show up. My mental capacity cannot handle any of it now. I will shut down, back up, and simply remove myself from anyone that tries to destroy my peace, period! We often think that it is impossible to remove ourselves from the negativity of any kind. But since I acquired courage, I have permitted myself to do so.

I find joy in the Lord in knowing that he is my peacemaker, and my peace is found in him. According to Matthew 5:9, Jesus says, *"Blessed are the peacemakers because they will be called sons of God."* Yes, Jesus sends us peacemakers, not someone that will pretend that their life is perfect but okay. Therefore, I learned that man cannot give you peace that only God can provide. Setting a goal and creating boundaries was necessary to obtain peace. I've learned to protect myself from the boldness of others that think they can just walk into my life and bring their baggage with them.

I had to gain wisdom and understanding over the loss I had endured during my life. It is as if I had to die as that person in order to find the other. We must remember that drama is unavoidable but hitting it off when it shows up is essential for a healthy lifestyle. I also learned that saying "No" to anything that caused me pain, frustrations, or fear was my God-given right. The word "No" can bring about a new meaning to you. I find satisfaction in saying "No" at times I am opposed to some people or things, and I am not intimidated by doing so. You might have to work your way up to it, but once you achieve that goal of saying it, you will be on your way to what God has in store for you. Remember to use it when necessary, as God still intends for us to be there for those that need us. In other words, I am now intentional about who and what I give my attention and time to while listening to the voice of God. I had to realize that everyone I met was not meant to fit into the space that God has created for me.

Life on the other side brought about a new type of freedom and allowed me to walk through an open door that nobody could close on me. It also gave me a renewed strength that now lies within my very being. I have obtained a new confidence, a light that has channeled all the darkness of my past. I grew free to do anything my soul desired, and I nurtured this ability. In addition, it filled me with the fuel to pull through challenges I faced and hide the scars of my past, both physical and emotional. I now have an impenetrable shield by living in the present moment. I gained confidence in the now, so much that I shocked myself. A moment that was once lost in time has found itself in the light of today, and it will never be dimmed again.

I did not realize then that I could be pushed through the storms to carry out the desires of my heart. All the desires that now occupy my present space, and yes, they were mine to keep. Who knew that my desires could be turned from tears of pain, to tears of belonging? I was missing in action. I had to find myself and help my daughter as well. The tears that helped me realize that what I had obtained was mine all along. Yes, mine to put in a frame of my choosing, and I chose one that was full of bright beautiful colors. The one that showed the essence of God. It captured all of my thoughts, emotions, and dreams. It was a frame that could not be broken by my past and had taken away all the guilt and shame. It was mantled ever so gently on a display of peace. I have mantled it in a place of light that cannot be overshadowed by darkness. Of course, It is now mantled in my heart with overwhelming brightness.

My heart shone with a brightness that was brilliantly seen through all the manifestations of my life's journeys. My journey now fills me with an awesome space that I thought I would never see. I used to imagine myself not living in this life because of the abuse. I began to live a new life that had silently erased my past. My emotions were enhanced by its presence in such a way that had me leaping for joy because I was now part of it. Leaping for what is to be and can grasp what is tangible because it's my time. I am now in a safe place of reassurance. Often my life's journey was altered by the shadows of the past. You know, the ones that would creep in every now and then? But now they serve as a new beginning and have a new meaning. A meaning that has found life to be meaningful instead of meaningless. A journey that has made me a Trail Blazer into my own future.

Your future must become more impactful than the torment of your past. Your journey will be full of new beginnings, and it should be a straight path versus a crooked path steered by someone else's emotions. It was my journey that allowed me to see the stranger as a stranger instead of the stranger I had lived as. You know that stranger you would see when you looked in the mirror? Yes, that stranger was me. It was then that I realized that domestic violence wasn't a journey, it was a wrong turn in life. A turn that lasted for a short period of my life, but had the impact of a major crash, and took a long time to recover from. I should have turned right when I instead turned left. Although I acknowledge that it took a toll on my life, I am glad I found a path to life on the other side.

Life has new meaning now and I can't understand how I was in that life for so long. I now realize I was held captive in a secure prison. That place that drew me into captivity of the unknown. I refused to stay on the merry-go-round of abuse, that cycle we stay on because of someone else's choosing. That life quickly crept up on me and held on tight to my emotional state. I now understand the hold it had on me. Was I blindsided into thinking that what I felt was true? Nope! The signs were there all along but gripped me so tightly, that it was hard to steer away from.

You must realize that life is a life worth living. That all mistakes are simply just that. I began to realize that life has so much to offer, and I deserved to have a part in it. I had to make up my mind and tell myself that what had captured me in a small moment of time does not capitalize on who I am or have become. Finally, I realized that all the scars became a turning point in the very direction I was destined to go. Once I figured out that, like a GPS that had steered me in the wrong direction, I found out you can quickly make a U-turn and set aside all the challenges of life. All the make-believe stories that I once told myself just to get through the day have now become my reality.

I can look back and see that it wasn't just myself that had to be set free, but the child I brought into a world full of deceit; a child that was innocent as the thoughts of peace, a child that loved me dearly and then started to retreat, child that was retreating within her own mind for safety and acting out emotionally for attention. Without knowing it, we were both

45

unwillingly caged. We were caught inside of a cage and crying to be set free. The child longed to be the child that was created to exist in a world full of sustainable challenges. A world that would not be full of fear and pain. I had captured the innocence of the child and boldly set that child free.

Innocence is the essence of life, a life given only by God. Innocence should be the freedom given to all. Your innocence should never be taken for granted. This is what captures the heart and soul of every child as they seek their right to survive. Innocence gets caught up in something that you did not create but carries the scars of many. It searches for the love that was promised and finally, it is in your reach. Love catches you by surprise as the warmth of it fills your heart. Like a flower, all the petals blossom that are sustained by the light. The light that draws you nearer to it and allows you to flourish with the beauty that you were meant to be. And finally, you are free.

Reflection: Making it to this point will sometimes seem so far away for some, but it will come eventually. Once you realize that life is worth living, there is so much more to you than what you realize. You will see that your battle has already been won.

"If your enemy is hungry give him food to eat; if he is thirsty, give him water to drink. VS 22, "In doing this, you will heap burning coals on his head, and the Lord will reward you."

Proverbs 25:21-22 (NIV)

CHAPTER 5: Finding Peace Through This Journey

Surviving domestic violence is a hard task on its own, however, it can be done. After all, my entire family survived it. The very first time that you see it, leave it. I remember thinking that I can't leave this marriage because the Bible speaks against divorce. I was trying everything to figure out how to get out of this relationship without sinning. I started going to a church that was of the Apostolic faith, which was my younger sister Crystal's church home. I started reaching out to her about the abuse that I was enduring, although I did not share the whole extent of it at the time. I couldn't be completely open about it because of the shame that came with acknowledging the abuse. More importantly, I was not aware of the term domestic violence, because no one ever talked about it.

We often see negative content regarding domestic violence on TV, for example, as I mentioned previously when there is a death that occurs related to domestic violence on the news or by word of mouth. Fear stops your progression completely. We instantly think that we are trapped in our situation as fear takes hold, because of what we just saw on the news or heard. I remember so vividly hearing about someone that I went to high school with being killed by her abusive husband on the news. At that time, I did not know she was experiencing abuse until her death. Her husband was let out of jail after being arrested for abuse, broke in through her back door, and shot her in the head while she was holding her child at the kitchen table. This took my mind to a dark place, putting more fear into my heart and mind, and kept me locked within my home where the abuse continued. I stayed in an abusive relationship because of that situation.

I came to realize that I could be that person because the abuse was just that bad that I was experiencing threats on my life. What I saw and heard from the news enforced that fear. Why aren't stories of survival ever shared on the news? We don't often see organizations that provide real assistance until interviewed when situations occur. During the time I was going through the abusive relationship, I knew of no organizations offering assistance.

Victims do not realize that others feel the same way that they do. Many don't even realize they are in the presence of another person that is or has been abused. The stigma of shame plays a huge part in what they will share and when. People like police officers, doctors, nurses, cashiers, construction workers, just to name a few, or even your best friend could be victims of abuse without you even knowing. One in three women experience some form of intimate partner abuse. It could not only be physically but mentally, sexually, stalking, financially, and socially such as social media. Victims are afraid to come out of the shadows and admit to anyone they are being abused. That was me! This also included family members. How could it be easy to admit that I was being abused? When outside of my home you would have thought I was the happiest person in the world. You could not tell that I was being abused at least from the inside. However, you don't realize that there are questions about your appearance that you may not even be aware of from people around you. I did not realize this myself, no matter the pretense someone was always wondering about the bruises.

I made excuses for the bruises and even hid them the best I could. Did I hide it well, or was that my true self? It definitely was not my true self, but I learned to pretend very well. The bruises would fade, but I could continue pretending to be happy. I couldn't answer that question honestly, but I can say that I truly loved that happy person that showed up and couldn't wait to see her any time she came around. She was a person who enjoyed laughter and having fun. Dressing up in her nursing uniform as she went to work and feeling cute was her joy.

Being able to show love to the people she took care of became how she survived. Outside of "The House", she was beautiful. Yes, my nursing career was part of what helped me survive. Even though I was not receiving my own help, I was able to help someone else. She also loved compliments because she never received them at home. The person that had given in to the abuse was only around when he was, or when she knew she was about to be in his presence. Oftentimes we hide our true selves when we are outside of what I call "The House" to fulfill a need that we miss.

We see ourselves vicariously living through someone else's happiness, if only for a brief moment but our minds eventually drift back to our own grim reality. One day, I had a conversation with my younger sister Crystal, and she reminded me about all the lies I told while being abused. Although she did not really know that then, she had a feeling about it. She recently informed me that at one point when she continued to see my bruises, she called my Uncle B for help. She stated that he came into town to visit and while here he monitored the abuser's every move.

While in town he never saw that side of him, my sister said. She was angry because she needed my uncle to take care of the situation at that time by any means necessary. She also stated that the abuser knew that my uncle was watching him. I learned that men that abuse will not confront another man the way that they confront and abuse women. I could not remember most of the events she was sharing with me from those years ago. Like, how I would lie and say I fell when bruises were spotted, or that I bumped up against something because of a black eye. There was always an excuse for the bruises that I had, as they showed up boldly on my light skin.

Although my family would notice things, they only had my word for what was going on to answer their questions. Had I lied even to myself about what my reality was? She reminded me of how I was protecting the person doing the abuse. We must stop protecting the abuser at all costs. I was permitting him to keep abusing me and didn't realize it then. I made so many excuses for the bruises with the rest of my family and acted like I was the happiest person in the relationship. In the privacy of my mind, I was calling out for someone to help me.

Now I don't know what phase of abuse I was in at the time, but it is never okay to justify any abuse, ever. It never dawned on me that my family could have helped me out of the abusive relationship early on. Why did I feel the need to pretend with them? Why did I feel ashamed to tell them what was going on in my home? Was I still trying to be the strong sister they looked up to when we were younger? Was I simply afraid to admit that fear had a grip on me? Whatever the case may be, your family are the ones that can shield and protect you when the need arises.

When I finally decided to leave, it was my family that I could trust not to disclose our location, even when my abuser showed up at their doors looking for us. Finding peace with the decisions you made during the abuse is a journey in itself. I look back and see so many ways that I could have been out. Why didn't I take them? Questioning myself is no longer an option, instead, I thank God for saving me. Again, if you see it at the beginning, leave it! I have come to realize that after talking to my sister that it is important to share with your family what is going on in your abusive relationship to have validation of your experience. This means that when you are the only one who knows your story, you are on your own to realize it and escape, but if you let others know, they can assist you and perhaps save others as well. Also, sharing your journey with family can also save their lives because they often can be caught up in the situation, and it will help them if they are informed. Abuse can risk the lives of the people around you as well. Remember I was denying the abuse. So, it is important to share information with someone you trust.

Ultimately, what we as victims have to realize is that we are more than enough. We are worth saving. We are who God created. He created us to be free beings, not abused beings. We were already predestined to be free before we were born. This means that we were not created by accident, but we have a purpose. Our lives have a purpose and it is not to be abused. *Zephaniah 3:17 (NIV)* states, *"The Lord your God is with you, the Mighty Warrior who saves. He will take great delight in you; In his love, he will no longer rebuke you, but he will rejoice over you with singing."* The way I interpret this scripture is that God loves us and finds joy in His creation. We have done nothing to deserve His love, but He loves us anyway. This scripture also says that we are to be loved by His creation and not abused. God does not intend for us to be beaten, cussed out, belittled, or frightened in any way. Oftentimes, I had to realize that peace belonged to me and no one had the right to take it away. I've often heard the saying "peace in the midst of the storm." I had to call on God often in the midst of my storms. Sometimes the storm in "The House" would be raging profusely, and shelter could not be found.

When everything appears to be chaotic, we must rest and know that God is there. Even in the times when I felt so exhausted to rest or sleep, I called on Him. Late in the midnight hours when I was afraid, crying, and sitting up in the middle of my bed watching over my child I prayed. I remember the night that my daughter called the police when she heard the abuse and the police officers showing up and placing handcuffs on the person that abused me for the first time ever, and when he left "The House" for the last time, my daughter and I played in my bed as I held her and we were able to rest knowing he could not return because he was in jail. I held my daughter close as we fell safely asleep peacefully for the first time. That is the kind of peace God has over our lives. Isaiah 26:3 (NKJV) states, *"You will keep in him in perfect peace, whose mind is stayed on you because he trusts in you."* Keep your mind on Jesus and peace will come. Philippians 4:7 (ESV) also states, *"And the peace of God, which surpasses all understanding, will guard your hearts and your minds in Christ Jesus."*

The bible speaks about Jesus calming the storm. It also speaks about Jesus being exalted and sleeping in a fishing boat while crossing the sea of Galilee at night. He was awakened by the disciples because they were afraid of the storm that had come upon them and nearly knocked over their boat. However, during the storm Jesus was asleep. Yes, Jesus slept through the storm. Therefore, we can overcome the storms as well and just sleep through them. Once awake Jesus calmed the storm by saying "Peace! Be still!", but then he rebukes the disciples saying to them *"Why are you so afraid"* asking them *"Do you still have Faith?"* (Mark 4:37-40). When I tell you what this scripture showed me about faith I am profoundly moved. My faith and beliefs are what sustain me to this day.

This is how God wants us to live, we are to find a place of peace through our journey called life. A journey that is honest and true. After crying for so long, it is time to follow that journey of peace. Leave the tears, fears, and the stigma of shame behind. Have you ever judged the journey you went through? Have you ever questioned God because of your journey? Have you ever listened to God's answer? I remember a pastor saying in a sermon many years ago when in the Apostolic faith that stated, "Why not you?" he was preaching about someone's journey of illness. The question we all have I'm sure is "Why me Lord?" This is meant for us to understand that we are not better than Jesus from having trials in our lives. Luke 9:23 says, *"Then He said to them all, 'If anyone desires to come after Me, let him deny himself, and take up his cross daily, and follow Me."* I took that to mean that no one is without a test, not even me.

Eventually, you will begin discovering your purpose through the journey. It may have opened up a lot of questions for you and may have even answered some. However, you may ask, "Am I good enough? Did I make the wrong decision again?" Finding peace through your journey allows the healing to come, and through healing comes purpose. Stand on God's word and His promises. I read a quote one day written by Pastor Clyde Posley of Antioch Church in Indianapolis, Indiana, where it said that God will break our heart early, so He can replace it with one like His, later. I found this to be a very profound statement. During this journey, I did find God, and with that came the understanding that man will break your heart. My heart was broken at a very early age, but God replaced it with His love. And His love can never be replaced as He promised to never leave us.

Reflection: Peace can mean so many different things to many people as to why they need it. However, it only means one thing to you. Allowing your Faith in God to help you find His peace is what will master your journey.

"Do not be anxious about anything but in every situation, by prayer and petition, with thanksgiving, present your request to God."

Philippians 4:6 (NIV)

Daisy Arness Marrs

CHAPTER 6: God Was There All Along

In our purpose in life, we are to show love and give love to others. That is the command from God. John 15:12 says *"This is My commandment, that you love one another as I have loved you."* Victims of domestic violence often forget their significance in life, simply because we have allowed ourselves to put trust in someone that does not love us. Love should not hurt, it's that simple. Don't allow deposits to be made in your life from someone else without addressing them immediately. Any negative deposits that we as women allow men to put into us take away from who we are, and who God created us to be.

When I think back to the relationship with my paternal father, I ask myself if I was willing to accept anyone that showed me attention because of the way he treated me. Did being abused become part of the norm for me because of how I grew up? I must reiterate that it was all I knew at the time. You only know what you know until you learn differently, right? 1 Corinthians 13:4-8 speaks about love stating, *"Love is patient, love is kind, it does not envy, it does not boast, it is not proud."* I had to understand, through the word of God, that the abusive relationship that I was in was not of God. This was not the life that was intended for me. Although God allowed it, it was not to become my final destination.

However, divorce was not supposed to be an option according to the church. You see, I joined a church of Apostolic faith with one of my younger sisters. Although I knew about God, I didn't really *know* God. This church taught differently than I knew from the Baptist church I was attending as a child. I learned about the gift of speaking in tongues, and I received the gift of the Holy Ghost while in the Apostolic church. Although I heard about those gifts, it was not part of what was traditionally done in the church that I grew up in. Being part of the Apostolic church, divorce was not an option. In fact, I was taught it was not an option in any church. I went to older Pastors in the church, and they were focused on men being head of the household.

The Bible also speaks against divorce so I felt like I did not have a way out. However, Matthew 19:9 states, *"And I say to you: whoever divorces his wife, except for sexual immorality, and marries another, commits adultery."* Was I learning that there was a way out through the adulterous relationship of my ex-husband from this passage? Yes, through the abuse was adultery as well. As I was looking for a way out of this abusive relationship in order not to sin, I continued my studies in the word of God. I came across 1 Corinthians 7;14-15 *"For the unbelieving husband has been sanctified through his wife, and the unbelieving wife has been sanctified through her believing husband; for otherwise your children would be unclean, but as it is, they are holy. Yet if the unbeliever leaves, let it be so. The brother or the sister is not bound in such circumstances; God has called us to live in peace,"*

Also, the book of Deuteronomy 21:11-14 speaks about divorce as well. I paid particular attention to this passage of scripture as it says, *"If you are not pleased with her, let her go wherever she wishes."* In addition, saying, *"You must not sell her or treat her as a slave since you have dishonored her."* This translates as "When a man chooses to be abusive, he breaks the covenant." Also stating, "An abusive man forfeits the right to remain married." Through my studies, God has revealed to me that he does not condone any type of abuse.

Many of us stay in abusive relationships simply because we think it is biblical, or for the sake of our children. What I realized much later in that relationship was the impact it had on my child, as staying affected her when she was more afraid of the unknown than I. When we know something in our relationship is not right, staying for our children is not an option, but only an excuse. I remember receiving a call from a particular teacher of my daughters when she was in the second grade. The teacher was telling me about how she was failing in class, and how she was not always attentive. It was at the end of a grading period, so I got upset with the teacher for not informing me of her concerns early enough for me to help my child. When I look back now, I should have known that what she experienced in "the house" was affecting her as well. She was so young and could not express her emotions. I didn't know how they affected her daily. I should have remembered how it felt from my own childhood, and the effect it had on my mental health.

Growing up, my siblings and I did not discuss what happened in our lives in terms of abuse until we were much older. After all, it was only when we were older that we had come to realize how wrong it was. One day, we all talked about it and realized that we were impacted in different ways throughout our lives. But emotionally, the effect on our psyche was the same. Eventually, I had to leave the church, because this was not the God I was truly learning about from my personal studies in scripture. The pastor did not seem to agree with divorce, no matter the situation. I began to spend a lot of time in prayer talking to God, reading His word, and believing it. God kept speaking to me, and I was listening. I had a revelation that God had been speaking to me throughout my life, even when I didn't know His voice. It wasn't until I learned about him through His words that I realized this.

Have you ever looked back over your life and thought about how you survived a situation? I remember falling out of a tree from about sixteen feet high at the age of nine or ten years old, and landing flat on my stomach. As other kids and I loved climbing trees, we would climb as high as we could to jump from the tree onto the top of old detached garages about two stories high. The higher we would climb the better. When it came to my turn to jump, I slipped and fell from the tree, all those feet, to the dirt as there was no grass that was waiting for me below on the ground. When I hit the ground, it was with great impact, and it knocked all the air out of me literally. It would take a while for me to be able to get all of my breath back as my stomach was sunken in towards my back. I remember my oldest sister Doris helping me up off the ground that day while panicking as she saw me gasping for air. The only thing she knew to do was assist me back home. We did not tell our mother about the incident, even though I sprained my right arm. Although I received treatment for the sprain, we didn't share with our mother how it happened until years later. After that fall, I became afraid of heights. How did I survive that fall? It was God who kept me that day.

There are so many situations that God brought back to my memory that made me realize that He was there all along. I also learned as a survivor, that victims of abuse often live in constant fear, which is the opposite of what God calls us to do. I also learned that God and fear cannot dwell in the same place at the same time. Just as light and darkness cannot share the same space. Psalm 27:1 says, *"The Lord is my light and my salvation; whom shall I fear? The Lord is the strength of my life; of whom shall I be afraid?* So how could they because God is love? When Jesus walked the earth, Satan tried his best to go after Jesus by tempting him according to Matthew 4:1-11. However, Jesus was able to stay within the light of the one that sent him, God his Father, and be without sin. Jesus did not fear the devil, but rather kept his eyes on God and the work that he was to do. He never wavered and fear had no hold on him. Therefore, fear is not to have a hold on us in any form. Knowing that fear and God can not dwell in the same space, how will you respond to it? 2 Timothy says, *"For God did not give us a spirit of fear, but of power, and love, and sound mind."* If God didn't give it to us, where does it come from? You guessed it; Satan loves to see us afraid because it is separating us from the love of God.

This made me pay attention because I was in constant fear. Fear of leaving the house, fear that my abuser would show up at my job because he had done so many times before, fear of being embarrassed in front of people I was around. Fear controlled my entire existence it seemed. What this meant to me was that I couldn't have faith in God to protect me and be afraid in my heart that He wouldn't. Psalm 5:4 states, *"For you are not a God who delights in wickedness; no evil can dwell with you"*. Therefore, since there was a lot of wickedness and evil going on in "the house", that I called home, my abuser did not belong there, or either my daughter and I didn't belong there.

We should also learn whether a situation is related to abuse or not if God isn't in it nor should we be. Ultimately, God started to reveal a lot of things to me in "the house" that did not belong there such as drugs and alcohol that contributed to the evilness that dwelled there. Once you start praying, God will reveal himself to you. Therefore, be prepared to have the truth revealed, and be prepared for what you will find out. Since God is truth, it is the truth that will come out. All the lies and deceitfulness will be revealed from your past, or even your present moment, and will have your head spinning. There is no other way, because your prayers and beliefs have *activated* the will of God. Remember, He will not interfere unless you invite him in. When I tell you God started to show up and show me a way out, He did. God revealed to me that He was not a part of what happened to me, it may have been allowed but it was not of Him. This reminded me of the book of Job and how God allowed Satan to attack him. Job 2:1-11.

The more I prayed and stayed in his word the more God revealed to me about the evilness that dwelled there. Although I didn't know it then, I realize today that Satan knew his days were numbered because of God's revelations to me. James 4:7 states, *"Resist the devil and he will flee from you."* This required a lot on my part because the dangers increased through the years based on what was being revealed. Did you notice I said years? You must first realize the wrongs in order to make them right, no matter how long it takes.

Satan was revealed to me, and that's when the abuse became even worse. I didn't understand that the more that you resist the devil and believe in the word of God, the angrier Satan becomes. He was losing his hold on me, and he was angry. Matthew 12:45 says, *"Then goeth he, and taketh with himself seven other spirits more wicked than himself, and they enter in and dwell there: and the last state of the man is worse than the first."* When I tell you those evil spirits showed up against me, they did. I would see the look of Satan through the eyes of my abuser, but God sent my guardian angels, and they were ready for battle. Ephesians 6:11-24 tells us to, *"Put on the whole armour of God, that ye may be able to stand against the wiles of the devil."* I had to put on the Full Armor of God, and the Shield of Faith became my protection. We are to look within ourselves and figure out our purpose and move forward with it. Domestic violence was not supposed to define who I was. It had shown itself for so long in my life, that it had to go. Once I realized this, a new awakening came for me to possess what was already given to me. Accepting myself also became major for me, because only then did I realize, that I mattered.

I remember losing my Auntie to domestic violence. My mother's youngest sister was twenty-six years old at the time of her death, but twenty-five when she started going through it. I was twenty-five years old once the revelation came to me that God did not intend for me to stay in a relationship of this magnitude. This revelation was revealed very vividly. Remember, I said God started showing up and showing out. It's as if God was speaking directly to me about the revelation of our ages, and if I didn't pay attention to Him when speaking, death would be my end result. I started paying attention, and I became very aware of my surroundings. He started pointing out things to me that were hidden within my home, and when He did, I didn't hesitate to act.

I remember a day when I came into "The House" and immediately God revealed to me a direction to go within my home. I was led downstairs to a particular place and when led to stop I looked up at an area in the ceiling, there was a small opening that I had not noticed before, and as I reached up inside of it there was a bag of drugs there. You can't imagine the look on my face. I was amazed that God's voice was so clear, but when He speaks, you better listen. God would often give me revelations after prayer, and indeed I would act. It was then that I learned that I had to be intentional and specific in prayer. It also brought back my conversation with God about my son, and how He listened when I asked Him to take him because of his sickness. Know that God is always listening! I am sure that many have heard to be careful what you pray for? I became very careful of what I had prayed for and spoke about from then on. However, coming out of an abusive relationship will take time and patience.

It felt as though I was always under attack at that point by my abuser, and unless I would give in to his demands, things would not work out in my favor. Therefore, I stayed in prayer, and I stayed vigilant to my surroundings. I had to maintain an act in order to live in my own home. Sheltering my daughter from most of the abuse became a major challenge, and I had to do whatever I could to keep her safe both mentally and physically. Although physically she was not in harm's way, I am sure she felt symptoms in her body from the fear she endured. She showed it in the way she would act out. But back then, I never put two and two together. The impact from fear does affect your body physically. Remember your safety and your children's safety is your top priority. Especially during the most dangerous time, when trying to leave an abusive relationship. You can find yourself in a life-threatening situation that can result in death.

Research has shown that the risk of more violence, including death is at the highest time when attempting to leave the abusive partner. Most often what we see and hear on the news of death related to domestic violence is because of someone trying to leave the relationship. Victims of abuse have to think beyond the pain in order to provide a means for a safe departure from their abuser. This may require months of planning or even years. Unfortunately, it became years for me.

I did not reach out to anyone in my family, and the court systems were not helpful when I sought assistance with my restraining order. Threats of violence put me in a paralyzing state in terms of leaving. I did not want to leave the home that I worked so hard for. I was thinking, "Why should I leave? He's the abusive partner!" At the time, I did not look past the material things that I had obtained. The Bible speaks on this. Luke 12:15 states, *"And he said to them, be on your guard against all covetousness, for one's life does not consist in the abundance of his possessions."* Was I putting material things over the will of God for my life? After all, He was constantly speaking to me and revealing things to me. I had forgotten that God had provided for me before, and He would do it again. Yes, I put material things before my life, though I was not realizing it at the time. It took me a while to realize that God was showing me who He was and that I could put all my trust in Him.

I found the place that God had prepared for me and surrendered what I was holding onto into His hands. I no longer wanted to hold on to the hate, bitterness, or material things that had occupied my existence because I found out that God was there - right beside me. Deuteronomy 31:6 says, *"Be strong and courageous. Do not be afraid or terrified because of them, for the Lord your God goes with you, he will never leave you, nor forsake you."* God has now drawn something out of me that I can't put back, and all my strongholds have been broken. The best example I can give is of a woman giving birth.

We are to carry the baby for nine months, and with that comes a lot of emotions, concerns, fear, pain, and then happiness. The waiting period seems very long as we anticipate the joy at the end of the journey. Finally, after months of waiting, we give birth and something amazing happens. Birth can be illustrated as releasing depression, fear, anxiety, and even surviving death. However, my illustration will be used with my two children that I gave birth to prematurely. I had to endure some extra hardships to fully develop. Things had to permeate for me to endure the suffering. It took more struggles, fears, anxieties, and a lot of uncertainty of what was going to happen next for me. But at the end, I fully received what God gave for me to birth, and there was beauty, joy, and happiness at the end of the waiting. That is what survivors want all along. We must come to realize that we are loved by the most-high God and when we seek His guidance, He will provide.

Reflection: God promises to love us even when we mess up. It's finding Him and abiding in Him that assures us of His presence. Trust in His word and know that He is God.

"So do not fear, for I am with you; do not be dismayed, for I am your God."

Isaiah 41:10 (NIV)

CHAPTER 7: Survival Mode; Changed Mindset

You may find yourself in a pretend situation, meaning you are pretending that you still love or care for your abuser to exit the relationship safely. This is hard to do because hatred is so strong towards the abusive person. This can take quite a bit of time and planning, depending on what your plans are. For example, you might be relocating to another state, finding a new job, or a new place to stay. To exit safely, we must prepare a safety plan in which social security cards, money, identification, and other necessities are put away secretly for our escape. It is often not necessary to share your plans, but it is important to share them with someone that can be trusted completely, such as family or trusted friends. I had a couple of friends that I could confide in and trust.

Keep in mind that this is often a run for your life situation. You must create a character within yourself to make it happen. It is hard to do this, but it must be done without making anyone aware of what you are doing. Most often we are dealing with an abuser that is a narcissist. A narcissist is someone that has no regard or little regard for those that are around them but focuses solely on themselves. In addition, they are not concerned about anyone else's feelings. I had no idea what this was while living in it with him. I had to create a character within myself to get out of the relationship with my life. I realized that the person I was trying to get away from cared nothing about me, it was all about him, so I was able to put up a pretense.

In paying particular attention to how this affects victims of domestic violence I was watching an episode of the *Red Table Talk* with Jada Pickett Smith. She was interviewing a doctor named Dr. Ramani. During this episode, Dr. Ramani described a narcissist as someone that is deeply insecure. They don't want to be found out, so they cover themselves in this grandiosity, entitlement, and arrogance. They have a lack of empathy, and to Dr. Ramani, this was the most lethal part of narcissists because they do not care that they are very controlling and paranoid. They think people are out to get them all the time. While in my abusive relationship I never knew any of this, but all the signs were there. What I needed or wanted was never a concern to him. However, I did learn to give in to the narcissistic acts without even knowing it to have peace. Dr. Ramani also spoke about "Grey Rocking." It is a term that I had never heard of before, but it was something I was doing while still in the relationship as well.

As I described above, I did anything to have peace. "Grey Rocking" is defined as disengaging from a narcissist to the point of being boring and uninteresting. When you start to disengage from a narcissist, they can become angry. I recall this as well, as this was the time when my abuser thought I was not giving him the attention he needed, and arguments would start. I found myself feeling as though I was on some type of roller coaster ride at times with all the ups and downs that I experienced during these cycles of abuse.

Dr. Ramani describes different types of narcissists, with the first one being Malignant Narcissists which are similar to a psychopath. These is psychologically dangerous, and sometimes physically dangerous people. In addition, she states that psychopaths are willing to lie, cheat, and harm you to your face without feeling remorse. This type of narcissist shows no empathy, shows aggression, and may threaten to leave. The person that is being abused will often end up apologizing, making excuses for their abuser and validating the abuser's feelings outside of their own, and blames themselves for the abuser's actions. Dr. Ramani describes this as the trauma bond, a strong emotional attachment to your abuser. As an advocate, my point of view would be not to ask the person that is being abused why they stay, and instead ask the abuser about his behavior.

Dr. Ramani, describes another type of narcissist called covert narcissist, in which they always are the victim, they blame everyone else and don't take responsibility, and their entitlement is quieter. We must realize that this is a cycle and you can never break them from it, so we must not validate their feelings and disengage from their conversations. We can't be enablers to narcissistic individuals.

Gaslighting is another trait that abusers have. Dr. Ramani explains gaslighting as a form of manipulation. I am sure that many of us have experienced this without knowing what it was. Have you ever doubted yourself with a narcissistic person? Let's talk about gaslighting. Wikipedia describes gaslighting as a form of psychological manipulation in which a person or a group covertly sows seeds of doubt in a targeted individual or group, making them question their own memory, perception, or judgment. I am sure we all know someone exactly like this. You may find yourself saying wait a minute, I know what I just heard or read. Have you ever been told "I never said that", or you feel as though you have to prove to the abuser that what you are saying is true?

If you ever feel like you have to bring in evidence, you are being gaslighted. When trying to survive domestic violence we often forget that we are the victims that need to be removed. I say this because we think, "What can I do to get him to leave or get him help?" Instead, we should remove ourselves from the toxicity of the relationship. It has to become no longer about the abuser and their behaviors. This is when survival mode comes into play, and a changed mindset has to take place. For so long it was about the person that did the abusing because I was trying to survive. However, understanding that I was the one that is in danger helped me realize that it was no longer about my abuser. I suddenly realized that I had to change my way of thinking. After being in an abusive relationship for so long I had to come to the realization that my own self-care was important.

Protecting my worth as a human being, and my child became my number one priority.

The hold that he had on my mind had to be broken. A shift was taking place and I had to be ready for it. Once my mind was made up, looking back was not an option. God was in charge at this point. I specifically remember telling my abuser that he would have to get me before I get him. I was tired and boldness was starting to show up. I felt like David when the scripture tells of how he used a sling and a stone to slay his giant. I was prepared for battle, and at all costs, I was determined to be the victor. I was tired and mentally drained, so my mindset had to change to survive. I remember I was walking down the street one day when a dog started to chase me. I remember looking around with nowhere to run, but I couldn't run because of the partial paralysis, anyway. I instantly took one of my shoes off and took a stand to protect myself. The dog backed off and I went home safe. This was the mindset that I put myself in to protect myself from the abuse, and with this strength I could survive the attacks that would come my way. There must come a time when you put your foot down and say no more. You have to be strong enough to understand that the battle is bigger than yourself. You must also know according to 1 Samuel 17:4, " *the battle is the Lord's...* " not yours. Therefore, don't allow yourself to be deceived into thinking things will get better without action, because they won't.

Reflection: Our minds and thoughts sometimes seem all we have. Don't let them take total control. We have the power to alter them at any time. Choosing what's right will help guide you through life.

"For I am the Lord your God who takes hold of your right hand and says to you, Do not fear; I will help you."

Isaiah 41:13 (NIV)

CHAPTER 8: If I Only Knew

This is the time not only to focus on your surroundings but to focus on what is ahead of you. You have to want freedom more than anything in the world and remember what you are doing is a temporary situation. It takes months or years to get from abuse to freedom. You must learn how to be the best actor around. You will continue cleaning the house, cooking, and doing all the standard routines as you prepare for a way out. You will be surprised to meet people along the way that have been in similar situations that you were in. Seeing that they are no longer fearful of a relationship that controlled their life gives you a new sense of hope that you have made it.

You may find yourself with tendencies of fear because of the situation you were in for so long as you adjust to your new life. I remember doing all of this to make it out of a dire situation. No judgment can come from any of this, because I did what was necessary to survive. I see it like "playing house" until the day comes for your escape. If I had only known what I know now, I would have been something to reckon with. I am more than a survivor; I am a conqueror. I am a strong, beautiful, and intelligent woman that is fearfully and wonderfully made. However, there were things that I went through first. Things would happen to my body that I wasn't prepared for. So many things outside of the bruising and pain that I went through are indescribable. Mental depression, symptoms of anxiety, insomnia, and Post Traumatic Stress Disorder (PTSD) would find their way into my life. Oftentimes you will not recognize these symptoms because they are masked by the fear that you experienced is what I determined.

During these times and afterward, as mentioned, some may experience periods of anxiety and or PTSD. These symptoms seem to appear out of nowhere. They began to take control of my life. Once I left the abusive relationship, I started to have feelings of panic and dread in the form of chest pains and a general feeling of uneasiness. I could not understand why. After all, I had a new job, met some new friends, had a new love interest, and was moving on with my life. I was at work one day at my new job, and I was happy because I had survived to make it through. Although at times my mind would worry that my abuser would find me. My body was not on the same page as my mind. I was wondering what were the symptoms that were attacking me to make me feel so afraid. They held a tight grip on me, and I found myself making several trips to the emergency room. I have since come to realize that those symptoms were remaining from the abuse, and they are called panic attacks.

A panic attack is a sudden feeling of acute and disabling anxiety, according to the dictionary. I became accustomed to all the different symptoms that attacked my body, and I didn't realize that my inner body was also under attack. Why wasn't I able to recognize these feelings before? I was not able to recognize them so prominently before because I was no longer in a fight for my life situation, and no longer had to fight or flee. This is the response that God has given us to protect ourselves when we feel we are in danger. Therefore, even though I was no longer running, my body had not yet gotten used to the peace that was provided for me. My body was still in that "fight or flight" mode. It had built up for years inside me, so it would take a while to get rid of. However, you can't get rid of what you don't recognize. I was still fearful of being found. While I was being this strong woman determined to move on, my mind was still in "the house" and back with the years of abuse.

How can you let go of years of abuse when you have escaped so suddenly? The years of abuse could not be turned off just because I was no longer in them. Was I fooling myself, or was I moving too fast in terms of thinking that I was happy? I think it was the latter. It makes me think of when we turn different ages. I remember talking to my daughter about something that I had read that made a lot of sense. Just because I turn a year older does not mean that I am mentally prepared for that new age. Although I escaped that relationship yesterday, this doesn't mean that I am mentally prepared to just move on today, without time spent in preparation.

Indeed, these symptoms were ones that I was experiencing in the abusive relationship all along. My body did not yet realize it had left, and so the symptoms continued to be there. My mind was still attached to those feelings that come when preparing to fight. Therefore, all those symptoms that I have felt for years became a semi-permanent fixture in my body for a while. I was also thinking how I would never go through anything like that again. That thought stayed with me for a long time. In all my perception, I was still there. Your mind feels what your body feels. I remember feeling those symptoms, and I remember how they frightened me once I was away from the abuser. I have now come to realize these were the feelings that were with me daily while protecting myself during the abuse. My body was preparing itself for battle, and it took me a while to realize I no longer had to. No counselor or therapist was telling me this. No one to make me aware of what I was feeling and what it was related to or how to deal with it.

After several trips to the emergency room, blood pressure elevated amongst other things. I thought I was having a stroke or something. It would be months of feeling these symptoms so I suffered for a while in silence when they would appear. I finally found a physician that sat me down, listened to me talk for about an hour, and informed me of what I was feeling and why. I was diagnosed with panic attacks. They silently appeared, about a month or so after I had found a new job, and moved on. If only I knew this when I first started feeling the symptoms, it would have saved me from a lot of emotional and physical trauma in my body from their effect.

In addition to the symptoms came questions. You may have come accustomed to hearing from others, "why did it take you so long to just leave?" That's when you shut down and stop talking about what you had experienced because it can often trigger you, and this can induce the panic attacks. Women that have not been in an abusive relationship need to understand that it isn't so simple to deal with. They don't understand being isolated from family, friends, or the mental abuse, while you have experienced the toll it has taken on your psyche. Why would you want to talk about something that caused pain anyway? Why would you want to talk about something that you left behind? They also want to make judgments towards you, as if they have never experienced anything themselves. Therefore, just know you owe explanations to no one. Finances also play a major role in staying, because the abuser may have been the sole provider. We do what we need to do. We stay! Many women think their situation will change even after experiencing years of abuse, and say to themselves things may get better. However, it does not take long for you to realize it will not change.

It is important to seek therapy to understand the trauma that you were in. I left that relationship and did not seek therapy for the trauma that my daughter and I had been in. It has been over thirty years and we still have triggers that take us back to "the house" where the abuse occurred. We often find ourselves talking about them and most of them I did not know affected my daughter. She should have received counseling, but I thought that because I got her out of it, she would be okay. Again, I should have remembered my experience as a young girl. It is important to be able to talk to someone professionally to be able to come out of the darkness as well as come to terms with what you and your family went through. In addition, you will start to see and understand things that you did not see during your relationship that you now question.

Questions will arise as to how you did not see what you were going through before, and how you allowed yourself to be put in a situation like you were in, or even how you allowed yourself to endure the abuse for so long once you realized it. Do not beat yourself up for it because after all what is done is done and we survived. We unfortunately cannot go back and change our past, but we can learn from it. You may remember thinking about the people that tried to talk to you about what you were going through, and why you were allowing it, but don't punish yourself for not listening. Why? Because you yourself can't understand it. There is no way that you can understand, let alone explain something that has turned your life upside down completely.

Just know that you owe answers to no one except yourself. Often, victims don't see themselves as being abused and make all sorts of excuses while protecting their abuser. They remember the days when they started dating and think back to when the abuse might have started. In the beginning, the jealousy the abuser portrayed comes off as cute, saying that he does that because he loves you, or maybe he wants to go everywhere that you go, and you think he loves being with you. He keeps you isolated from friends or family and you thought he loves being with me just that much more and wants me all to himself.

These were small tell-tale signs that I missed myself even after being hit for the very first time while in high school. I can also ask myself, "How did I miss the abuse I was in, or how did I just accept it?" After all, I saw my mother experience abuse when I was a child. Therefore, did I just put it in my mind that this is the way it is supposed to be? Here comes the big question. Are women supposed to be abused by men? We see abuse of women where they are being smacked around in movies on television, we hear the abuse in songs, we even see most women accept how women are demeaned in the music today. We also have seen police officers abuse women on the streets.

Did you know that police officers have a high incidence of domestic violence towards their mates? According to statistics, "Studies have shown that 40% of families of police officers have experienced some type of domestic violence." Also stating, "This can include harassment, stalking to homicide." (Michael A, Gottlieb, PA) Victims want to be able to trust the people we call for help while being abused. I am thankful that the officers that showed up at my home were there to assist me. I remember a police officer showing up at my door one day, and when I answered the door I had no idea why he was there. When I opened the door, the first thing that he asked me was if I was okay. I said yes, but then he slightly shifted to the side and silently whispered asking me again. Are you okay? Although I didn't know why the officer showed up at that moment, I had learned that a neighbor had called the police because my ex-husband was lurking around the back of my home. I wish I knew that at the time, because my neighbor didn't phone me to let me know. I honored first responders once I started my organization because they assisted in saving my life. They came into my home to take me out of a dangerous situation, with no hesitation.

I saw it in my own home growing up when they came after me and my siblings with our mother. I have come to learn that we have the power to change our destiny. We should not get caught up in what was, especially what we went through in our childhood. Too many times you hear people talking about how they blame their father, a teacher, mother, or someone else for what they have gone through while growing up. I have done that myself until recently I had to question myself. How can you blame someone else for what you know? We know what's right and what's wrong, and someone else's wrong doesn't have to define us. You may not know that at first, but once you do, you can change. In addition, how can you allow yourself to live in a reality that was never yours anyway? Your past is something that you allow if you continue to dwell there. You allow someone to continually bring you pain if you don't grow beyond it.

We have the power to change situations, but we have to know how to recognize them. It's called growth, and learning who you are will help you move beyond someone else's choices. The choices my father made may have shifted my life, but I have the power to alter that direction. I had to forgive him to find myself. While speaking about forgiveness, how can you expect to be forgiven by God if you don't forgive? Hebrews 8:12 says, *"For I will forgive their wickedness and will remember their sins no more."* Therefore, the bible is telling us to remember and sin no more. It also tells us we can be healed. After speaking with my siblings, I realized that the course of my life was altered, when the abuse I witnessed at a young age helped me to survive my own. Because of this, I was able to leave my relationship alive.

Women that are abused often hear the question? "Why don't you just leave now? I will help you." Maybe it isn't as simple as just walking out the front door. Women that say they haven't been abused, don't often realize that they have been. I have heard many women say that they have never been physically abused, but will admit to being cussed out, yelled at, and even financially and sexually taken advantage of. This is a form of abuse! However, women who are abused are torn between leaving their home or staying to make the relationship work. Although these tactics have been tried so many times before we know in reality it won't work. Victims of abuse often blame themselves and must realize it is not their fault. Victims must not feel they are the cause of the way someone else acts or treats others. It is only our fault if we allow it to continue. Therefore, you can realize that the situation you are in is not safe. You can understand that someone that only thinks of themselves on a first date, as being a red flag for you.

Isolation is also another tactic that abusers use to try and retain control. Most often the victim doesn't realize how much they have missed out on in life until they come out of an abusive relationship. When I was in an abusive relationship the abuser lived life as usual, coming and going as he pleased while I was at work or home. This is no way anybody should live, but this is what happens. I regret missing so much in my younger years, and I used to get angry about it. Manipulation was a major part of the control that was over me. Manipulation is defined as the usage of psychological influence over a person or situation to gain an outcome. Does this sound familiar? It was something that may have been short-lived like saying something that he thought I would want to hear to stroke his ego. It was never about me though.

Once victims of abuse have left their abusive relationship safely and are preparing for a new life, realistic goals need to be put in place. What does this mean? At this point, you must realize that you must find out who you are, because your identity is no longer attached to your abuser. Your abusive relationship allowed him to control your very being. First, we must discover ourselves all over again. For many survivors, learning yourself for the first time proves difficult after living in a twisted reality for so long. What are your likes and dislikes? Do you even know? Who are your friends apart from the abuser? You may have to learn who your family is all over again. You have been "missing in action" so to speak and adjusting to the small things may become a daunting task.

You now get a chance to see God's true creation, "yourself". You re-learn the beauty of your smile, the way you want to wear your clothes, or even how you want to style your hair. After being controlled for so long all of this becomes an important factor to your new identity. You may tell yourself you are still the same person when, in actuality, you are not. Let me explain. For as long as you were in the abusive relationship you identified with your abuser. For example, you couldn't wear certain types of clothes, you couldn't wear makeup, or you couldn't do certain things. It may sound crazy to use the word "couldn't" but that is what many experience. They became accustomed to it. Those things that would trigger the abuser because he thought you were wearing things for somebody else. To keep the peace, you gave up your identity. You gave in to his powers. It makes me angry just thinking about it. How could I have given in to someone like this! Like many victims, I was surviving. It is so important to understand your boundaries, because repeating any of this is not an option.

According to the Bible, God created man and woman. I believe we are God's greatest creation. What this means to me is we are perfectly made in his image, and because of this fact, we are beautifully and wonderfully made. Remember that crown that I talked about? Now it can be adorned in so many beautiful ways. Therefore, now that you have found a way out of that relationship, your beauty should shine bright. Not only in body image but in personality as well. You must begin to love who you are becoming. Start by building your self-esteem up. It's time to show up and show out.

Also, begin to set boundaries for yourself. Setting boundaries will be one of the most important things to accomplish. Set goals for your new life and fulfill them, and don't worry about setting time limits. Setting realistic goals will be more gratifying and less stressful. It is now time to just sit back and enjoy the ride, as they say. This is an exciting time for you and the skies are the limit, because your life has changed drastically for the better. You will face challenges at times, everybody does, but don't let that slow you down. View them as minor setbacks and keep moving forward. Enjoy every single milestone that you accomplish and celebrate each one of them.

Knowing that you have control of the present moment will bring you to a place of peace, eventually, and because you know that you can control it, this will help you reach your goals. If only I knew a lot of things regarding trauma from abuse I was going through, it would have saved me and my daughter a lot of unnecessary pain. Don't be afraid to investigate someone, do your research, and if something doesn't feel right or sound right from the start, that's probably because it isn't. Always know your worth and trust your instincts. Finding your true self is going to be more rewarding than you can ever imagine. Don't sit on the side lines, be intentional about life and enjoy it.

Reflection: Knowing who you are is essential to development in life. It is what often steers us and guides us through. Learning God's truth will help you separate the truth from false narratives.

"Pride goes before destruction, a haughty spirit before a fall."

Proverbs 16:18 (NIV)

Daisy Arness Marrs

CHAPTER 9: No Longer on the Run

How is it that we have come to a situation in our life that we feel that we have to run from something or someone to escape abuse? I remember thinking about this very question. My abuser was trying to attack me one day. All I can remember was grabbing my daughter and my car keys, running out of my house, and getting us in my car as fast as I could. We made it to the car so fast my adrenaline was at an all-time high. This is the fight and flight that I was speaking of in the previous chapter. I knew the symptoms were there but didn't realize it until after I was out of the abusive relationship. Anyway, my daughter and I made it to our car, and I sped off. It had to be God that didn't allow the abuser to catch us, because I didn't know he was going to follow us close behind. We were in a high-speed chase, and this was very much like you would see on the movies or television. I drove for a few miles with him tailing us the whole time. I tried everything to get away from him, I took a quick turn in a park and continued trying to lose him, but he was still driving close behind.

Suddenly, a police officer was coming from the opposite direction. I swerved my vehicle to get the police officer's attention and waved my hand at the officer and he turned his lights on. I was able to let the officer know that I was being chased by the car behind me and informed him that it was my abuser. In addition, I explained to the officer about the restraining order I had on him. With my abuser following close behind me, there was nowhere for him to go, and the police officer was able to stop him. No arrest was made that day, but that was the day I said I was no longer on the run. Why should I keep running when I'm not receiving any help? I am not running anymore.

I had realized that it was going to either be him or me. And I had to mentally prepare myself for battle. How was I going to protect myself against the unknown of where and when my abuser would show up? When would the time come that I would have to fight for my life? Survivors of abuse are often filled with this sense of dread, where fear would give them strength or courage that they didn't know they had. I remember being told from my mother and other relatives that my grandfather was working under a car when something slipped and the car fell on top of him pinning him underneath. He was unable to free himself and was in a dangerous situation. My grandmother was frightened but instead of running for help she found her inner strength and lifted that car off him. She freed him and saved his life. When fear strikes you, you can find the strength to survive. God gives us strength when He knows we need it. That was how I felt that day, because I knew there was no one helping me or my daughter.

There were many times that my daughter and I would get home late at night because I worked the late shift, and I had to pick her up from whoever was watching her. It would be dark outside when we got home most evenings, so I would make sure that it was safe for us to get out of our car to go into the house. I would shine bright lights from my car onto my home, and because our driveway went around to the back of the house, I would also drive around to make sure no one was lurking. After all of that, I would go into the house alone while leaving my daughter in the car to check everything out before allowing her to come into the house. It was a "catch-twenty-two" for me in choosing to leave her in the car alone while going inside our home alone, as both options frightened me. However, if the abuser was inside, or anyone else was in our home, I could not allow her to be with me. I kept a knife with me in the car and would take it with me for protection when checking inside the house.

Keep in mind that the restraining order that I had obtained did not allow the abuser to stay at our home or come within so many feet of my daughter and me. I thought that I could not continue to be a prisoner of my past. Typically, life should be as we imagined it to be, right? When we were kids, we had dreams of what we wanted to be when we grew up. We talked about who we would marry and probably talked about having babies. Our dreams should have become our reality. However, as we get older some things change and some of our dreams never come to pass. After all, we were just kids. I truly believe that without knowing, my father changed my destination for me because of the abuse. Even though I had dreams of happiness as a child of the man I would marry, what I lived through with him attracted the same kind of man that abused me.

Once I realized that I was more than my abuse, my life started to change. And yours can too. You can break free from your past. You can choose to no longer live there. Joyce Meyer said it perfectly in her book, *Battlefield of the Mind: Winning the Battle in Your Mind, page 23,* when she stated, "Our past might explain why we are suffering, but we must not use it as an excuse to stay in bondage." I realized that I was a single mother with a child to protect. I could not allow my child to continue to experience the abuse alongside me. Statistics say it often takes victims of abuse at least seven times to finally decide to leave their abuser. Also, statistics say that children that experience abuse as a child may have ongoing problems emotionally.

Now that the decision I made was profound enough, the situation changed my life. How could I continue putting my child through this? How could I continue running from a situation that could lead to the end of my life? Letting go of the once was and indulge in the life that God has created was where my mind drifted to. Moving forward meant that my past no longer had a grip on me, and I was no longer going to be pulled back into a situation that God had freed me from. Being on the run was no longer an option for me, as I was once held captive but now, I'm free.

I wasn't going to make the mistake again that gave my abuser the opportunity to attack me. Once your mind is in survival mode, you will do anything to protect yourself. I was becoming like my mother in that moment she was courageous enough to show up with the police to retrieve her children. She had gotten tired of running, tired of fighting, and tired of crying. Her escape had turned into a part of survival. That day, she became a woman instead of a girl in fear of the man she called husband. My mother became bold enough to leave my father. She may not have been a superwoman, and she did remain angry over her circumstances. Maybe she had reached the seventh time or maybe the fifteenth time, but what mattered is, she reached the breaking point and knew it was time to go. The battle that she had prepared for had shown up and given her strength to fight, to live.

It is essential that you also get to this point. The abuser can stand against someone that is not prepared to fight, but once you are prepared, things take a change. However, you must remember that safety is always the key. It should always stay front and center in your mind. Once the battle is over and you reach the end of your journey, there may be some things that you need to tidy up. As you venture out into finding your new self, don't let others tell you who you are. This will become an exciting time for you in finding that out for yourself. You will enjoy finding a new reason to run as you strut into your new journey called life. The anger that once accompanied you will be sent to the wayside as you begin to appreciate a new life and love. You are now giving yourself permission to move forward, by not allowing past failures, circumstances, relationships, and people that weren't made to fit into your life in the first place. New doors will be opened, and with that comes new challenges, but it will be up to you to meet them. Don't let anyone change your destiny from this point on. Only allow the will of God to control you now. In addition, don't become distracted by others you may see as being "ahead" of you. You will reach your own goals in your own life's unique circumstances. So instead, walk boldly into your life as if it was always waiting for you.

Reflection: Separating the dark from the light will help us understand which direction we are to go. Once we can do that, we will not walk on a lonely path.

"Let us then approach God's throne of grace with confidence, so that we may receive mercy and find grace to help us in our time of need."

Hebrews 4:16 (NIV)

CHAPTER 10: Life Beyond the Shelters

When going through domestic violence, I was not aware of shelters at the time. While in the court system filing divorce papers and obtaining a restraining order to protect my daughter and me from my abusive partner, I was not made aware of shelters that assisted victims with temporary housing. However, I learned that shelters take you beyond the pain of abuse and give you a place to stay safely away from your abusive partner. Although shelters are a safe haven, what comes next? What is life beyond the shelters? How do I let go of my past and move beyond the shelters? How did I get here?

While listening to a sermon by Pastor Touré Roberts, he stated something to the effect, "You may not be able to reshape your past, but you can re-spin it. With every temptation, God gives a way of escape. There is a trap door to the right if you are willing to go, but there is always a door." This spoke to me, as if the message was simply for me. This was the message that God was speaking to me about. While our flesh is a temporary shelter, there is a permanent place for us. I found myself afraid of the temporary solutions, because I did not know about the permanent or how I would arrive there. Although the temporary shelter may be beautiful, it can fall apart. It does not belong to me, and eventually I would find a permanent place. The shelter is a temporary escape for those seeking refuge from their abuser, but there is an exit door.

I remember the words that God gave me: "A way out is available from the Lord. He opens all the exit doors that Satan has stood before, a way out is available from the Lord." God is telling me that Satan tried his best to block a way out for me. However, those doors were open when I was given an opportunity to go through it. If you listen to His voice, God will guide you through as well. Even though I was not aware of shelters, I found my door. My shelter was a place hidden within myself, but this was not enough. I had to find a physical place that I realized God had given me as a way out. It allowed me to peel off the old and shed everything that had held me and my daughter back. As shelters are meant to be temporary places, so are relationships of abuse. In fact, they were never meant to be at all.

When I left the abusive relationship and moved into my first place, the peace that I felt could not be explained. It gave me and my daughter space to breathe and think. It also allowed me to find private time to reflect on the past and plan for our future. Although it was a temporary place, it provided us safety and security. A townhouse apartment gave me and my daughter shelter, without them knowing we were running. After being there for only six months, it was time for us to relocate again. The happiness that we shared in that moment was unexplainable. People that don't understand what victims of domestic abuse go through will not understand the excitement in going about your home with no fear. Leaving a shelter and moving on with life gives you a sense of empowerment. In quoting Pastor Touré Roberts again he stated, "You feel confident and feel good, this thing that once had me now is under my feet." I found myself shouting on that statement alone. It was time for us to make room for the present.

The place of shelter gave us the ability to find ourselves and allowed us to start our journey of healing. Living in our temporary shelter also helped me understand what my daughter and I went through. We did not have the opportunity to think about ourselves during times of abuse. We enjoyed discovering who we were beyond it, and I loved the person that I had come to be. Leaving the apartment, our temporary shelter led us into our future and helped us figure out what we needed in life beyond the abuse. I did come to realize that staying in that first home I purchased was to prevent us from being homeless. As long as I stayed in the home, I was able to receive mortgage assistance from someone near and dear to my heart who passed away eventually. However, at the time, she was over the Center Township trustee's office and looked out for me. She knew why we needed the assistance. It was from being out of work for almost a year due to the injury to my back.

Today I realize that there is nothing, not even the possibility of becoming homeless that should have kept us living in that house. Some agencies will and can assist you from that very possibility. Advocates for victims of domestic violence are great resources in assisting you with getting beyond the barriers between you and a shelter. Just get in touch with your local agencies in your state for assistance, and they will be there to help you. In addition, seek counseling as this is very important and will help you move forward from the mental and physical trauma experienced. Find a home that will become your safe place. A home that will help you look beyond the pain of abuse to create new memories. When decorating our new home, I loved the fact that I made my own choices of what I wanted in every room as each new piece provided peace.

Decorating became a part of the healing process for us, as it helped disconnect us from our past. New photos were put up and the old ones were put away. I remember the first night that we were in our new place and the peace that we had when going to bed. When I tell you God's peace is better than anything, it is. Being able to go to sleep without being awakened from abuse, was unexplainable. Waking up the next day with smiles on our faces, knowing we were safe, made us realize how far we had come. Each day became a new accomplishment, almost like a new adventure. We loved dancing and singing to songs that brought us joy in our new home. We were finding our new identity and were able to fix our brokenness.

Making room for yourself, is a major accomplishment. What does that mean? For me, it meant finding myself in the moment, establishing what is meant for me right now. Not worrying about my past or what tomorrow brings, especially since we are not promised tomorrow. Living in the moment gives us clarity of our now. Since the present moment is all that we have, let's celebrate as we were thankful for our present shelter. The joy that lies within each room is my life beyond the shelter and my past. What will yours be? Will it contain your past, or will you allow life beyond the shelter to give you a new direction towards your destiny? Temporary places are just that, temporary. And as we found our permanent home, we never forgot those precious moments we had together in our temporary space. We were then able to separate the distractions that came with our old way of living, and it helped us find ourselves.

Reflection: There are many places that we can call home, but there is only one place that can bring you joy. Finding yourself is one of the most powerful experiences in life, because in doing so you will find your true home anywhere.

For you have been my refuge, a strong tower against the foe. Vs 4 "I long to dwell in your tent forever and take refuge in the shelter of your wings."

Psalm 61:3-4 (NIV)

Daisy Arness Marrs

CHAPTER 11: Triggers Will Come
(Understanding Where I am Through the Phases of Abuse)

I was at work one day in my office. A man from the therapy department came to visit. I can't recall why he came or what the conversation was about, the only thing I could focus on was his tone of voice. While trying to talk, he became angry and raised his voice. This triggered me and sent me to a place of remembrance. I mentally prepared myself for another battle. Warfare was about to take place, the fight and flight reaction was activated, and I refused to allow that man to control my space. All of a sudden I was in a room with this man all alone and felt a sense of dread come over me. All these emotions started coming back. I remember the tears that I shed and the need to protect myself. I was not going to let this man control the situation. I demanded that he leave my office, and I was very loud about it. I was so loud that my direct supervisor from across the hall came into the office. The Executive Director also entered my office after being called by my supervisor. The therapist continued to speak rudely and wouldn't leave. I remember the Executive Director entering my office and taking control of the conversation with the therapist, and he attempted to speak rudely to her as well.

Yes, the Executive Director of the facility was female and a person of color. The man from therapy was a white male and spoke as if he had authority over her and me. However, not even realizing that she was protecting me emotionally at the time, she took complete control of the situation, shut him down, and gave him the choice leave my office or the building. He chose to leave my office. As I look back on that situation, I realized women can have the authority over someone that thinks that they have power over us. It is all about the position we take on it. Nicole spoke with authority, and at that very moment she was in charge, and I believe it wasn't because of her position she held at work, but the position she took at that moment as a woman. Although she had direct authority over him, it was her stance that showed authority. I was in a different position as someone who had experienced abuse, but I learned something from her that day. If we take the position of not feeling threatened from the beginning, we too can have that control over a situation. When you find yourself in a similar situation, take complete control over it, no matter your position.

After he left my office, my immediate supervisor and the Executive Director tried to talk to me to figure out what was wrong, as the tears were still falling from my eyes. They wanted to know what was really going on. I was unable, at the time, to share with them that I was a survivor of domestic violence, and the man had triggered my emotions. He had taken me back to a place of verbal abuse that I had experienced. Many people would not understand it anyway. He also was standing by my office door, and I felt trapped with no way out at the time. I had not known our new Executive Director very long because she was new to the position, but she came up and hugged me, and it made me feel safe.

Triggers are something that brings back trauma or memories to a victim of domestic violence, and they can be very traumatizing or debilitating. A day or so later, I felt as though I had to go to the Executive Director and explain to her why I had gotten so emotional. The name of that Executive Director was Nicole Fields. I recall going to her office to speak with her after getting up the nerve to do so. She welcomed me in and made me feel a sense of calm as she offered me a seat in her office.

I was feeling terrified just thinking about talking about my experience. Survivors of domestic violence often feel ashamed and embarrassed. They don't want people to view them differently because of their past experiences. I was feeling very vulnerable at that moment. Oftentimes, survivors are judged, even when they are currently going through domestic violence, as to why they allow themselves to deal with situations like that. Why do you stay? How can you let someone treat you that way? Those are the questions that victims don't want to hear. As I sat in her office, I informed her that I wanted to share with her the reason behind what happened during the encounter with the therapist.

It was important to me that she understood because she showed compassion for me that day and protected me during a situation without being aware of it. Nicole was very understanding, and it seems as though we talked for a couple of hours. She allowed me to share openly with her my experience of being a victim of abuse, and she didn't mention the work that I should have been doing at the time. She listened to me intentionally, and that was so important. I found myself in a judgment-free zone and unashamed to share my story with her. It is not often that you can find someone that you can trust at work, especially the person that is in charge of the entire building, but I trusted her with my information that day. We created a bond that I can't explain, and I was able to be myself from that day on, knowing she would be there to listen. She would also protect the information that I shared. Nicole was a counselor in my time of need, she listened and shared her own thoughts.

My daughter and I did not receive counseling after our trauma, as I was never made aware of the need for it during my divorce. It would have been so important in helping us move past what happened. I have many regrets, and not taking my daughter through counseling was one of them. I should have been receiving it myself at the time as well. Don't make the same mistake, and don't think that you can get through this all alone. We make decisions based on our past to avoid our triggers. Sometimes my daughter speaks to me of triggers in her life, and it saddens me because I did not think she would have them. In fact, I was not even aware of them myself. Whether it's a sound she hears in the night, a job that she has, or even just seeing me in pain, things will trigger her back to the past of what we both went through. She was all I had, and I had to protect her. I am sure everyone understands what I am saying as a mother. Recently, after the murder of George Floyd, women all over the country heard him call out for his mother. The reaction from a lot of us when hearing him call out for her was the response of a mother, from our deepest instincts. We are supposed to protect our children.

My daughter and I have an amazing bond. I often find myself being her counselor, or she may be mine. She is a very strong-minded and determined young lady. I love her confidence and how she applies herself. After all, I did not want anyone taking advantage of my child under any circumstance. Oftentimes, I tell her she walks with authority. Many people have misjudged my daughter and me, until they got to know us. After the abuse, I wanted to make sure she presented herself as a strong, trustworthy individual with a lot of confidence in everything she applied herself in doing. I taught her to protect her feelings, and to be cautious of how others treated her. I told her it was important to be true to her word, and to be honest. Also, I made sure she knew to never let someone take advantage of her, like what happened to me for so long. Number one on the list, was I wanted her to protect herself at all costs. Because of these lessons, people would take her approach the wrong way. They believed she applied her confidence in the wrong way, until they got to know her. I taught her to be built for better, so that she would not follow the footsteps of abuse.

We hear women aren't supposed to be strong and confident, especially in a man's world. I also find people intimidated by a strong-willed woman, especially one of color. You hear that a lot. Don't let people belittle you just because you have built yourself to be better as a woman, no matter your skin color. Be aware of your triggers because they will come, and when they come, walk through them with grace, and don't be afraid to find someone that can be your place of safety. I remember meeting another person at the same job I worked with Nicole. She was from our corporate office and was a very inviting person. She did not use her title to intimidate people. I often found her protecting me, without her even knowing it. Her name was Gina Auker, and we were also able to establish a great working relationship. She was not judgmental and I felt her passion in how she cares for people. She intentionally listens and wants to help employees be the best they can be. As a nurse herself, her compassion was shown in other ways as well.

My daughter and I worked as nurses at the same facility. She wanted to follow in my footsteps career-wise. I would often take her to work with me when she was a little girl and my passion rubbed off on her. A personal relationship was established between Gina, my daughter, and me. Although she did not understand our story at first, she ultimately came to realize it. After a family who was very close to Gina, experienced a tragic loss, she shared their story in an event with our organization, and it was there she found out what my daughter and I had experienced. As stated in a previous chapter, it is important that employers know their employees as people, and the reasons behind who they are. What I found most comforting, is that they got to know my daughter's story and her reasons for being the woman she is today. I think God sends people in our lives for a reason, no matter the circumstance. My daughter and I needed people like Nicole and Gina at work, even though they didn't realize it at the time.

Remember that there are different phases of triggers at different times in your life that may show up at different times. It could be emotional, physical, financial, sexual, or even certain sounds that may cause you to relapse by taking you back to a certain moment of abuse. However, there may be people that can help ease them along the way. One of the triggers that affects me today, is seeing a knife lying around on a kitchen counter. It will give me a slight chill, simply because I had a knife placed in my back. I've learned to allow myself to feel the emotion, put the knife away, and then let it go through recognizing the trigger for what it is. Learning preventive measures and the process of recognizing triggers are the first steps toward managing them. Talk to yourself if it helps.

Whatever you decide to do, do not let the triggers continue to give your abuser a hold on your life. It didn't take me long to realize this myself because when triggers come, they take me back to an emotional place with my abuser. I refuse, after many years of freedom, to continue this cycle by giving him power over me. I can't even remember the particular date that the most traumatic injury happened in my life, and I am so glad that I can't. In a small way I was remembering him. Now, I give myself permission to release and let go. Embrace the new you and help yourself build up a defense against the past. Talk about it and allow yourself to be strong in the moment. Feel the natural feelings and know what they are and what you must learn in order to move on. It's still a process, even years later.

Reflecting only on what was positive when you came out of your relationship like the strength it took to leave, is a good step. But don't focus on the negative because you will allow the abuse to continue to affect and control you. I had to understand that principle because every time I was in pain, I would reflect on the reasons from the days of my abuse. I would remember why I couldn't wear a particular shoe. It would take me right back to the feelings of abuse. The anger would come, and right behind it was the symptoms of anxiety, because of the fear that came with it. This is why we must move forward. Instead, I say thank you Lord that I can feel the pain, thank you Lord that I am still here, and thank you Lord that I can walk and then move on from there. This will require some mental adjustments on your part, but you can get there. Remember there's a whole lot of you that needs to experience what life has to offer, beyond the abuse.

Here's an example. My grandson was given a project at school to allow a butterfly to develop. He was given a Pupa as a chrysalis, the beginning stage of a butterfly. For days, he had to watch the development of the pupa as it went through its stages. It seemed to him that it was taking a long time to develop. However, it was hard for him understand that inside the pupa something beautiful was going on. After a couple of weeks, a caterpillar emerged from it, but it wasn't finished yet. Eventually, after all the stages were complete, a beautiful butterfly was sitting in the little cage. Although he didn't visually see what was happening as it was going on, there was a process that God was working on. The same slow process happens as we fight through our triggers. They are gradually taking a new form in our minds through our thoughts and actions. God is creating us to be new creatures. It's something that you can't see until the beauty of freedom emerges, and just like that butterfly that was able to fly out of his cage, you will also be set free. Like the butterfly, you will find yourself as something beautiful when it eventually emerges, and you will not allow yourself to be caged anymore.

Because we worked together, my daughter would be able to come to me when she needed to find a safe place at work. Together we experienced triggers that only we knew about and could talk about with each other. It could have been how someone spoke to her or treated her that would trigger her emotions. Her triggers were always emotional, she was not physically abused, but witnessed the abuse that I endured. In learning about triggers you will find it is okay to talk about them, but never okay to dwell in that moment. They will torment you and send you spiraling to a place that you left if you allow it. For a moment, you will be back in a place of darkness. This is part of the cycle of abuse, because not only would I relive the moments they would be so vivid to me. I questioned many times why things would continue to haunt me after so many years. I learned that triggers from abuse may last a lifetime if you allow them to. I can be watching a movie, and the events of my past would come to mind. Again, staying in that moment would be self-torment.

My husband does not like watching certain types of movies related to abuse, but sometimes I would find some sense of therapy in them when the woman would get revenge. Emotional abuse is something that survivors experience and don't realize, even after we leave our abusive relationship. Thoughts are sometimes generated by how we feel. We may try and display that through conversation with someone. So, when you are sharing your concerns or feelings with someone, no matter what it is, you want to feel validated. I want to be heard whether I'm at work or in my home. It is very important to me, because during the abuse I was not heard at all. Triggers may come when I don't feel as though I am being heard or my feelings validated. However, something might not be to my liking, and it may trigger something from my past, but it is not my past. Now I have to pull myself out of that state of mind, to deal with the moment in a positive way. This allows me to understand that what's going on in the present is not connected to any form of abuse but is just a typical emotion that comes with basic conversation. Therefore, my validation during a conversation does not have to come from the person that is listening but from myself.

Learning how to live after abuse is hard because too often, reflecting while in the present moment takes me into the past. Someone may say something with a different meaning than the person that abused you, but what you hear is something you have decided not to tolerate anymore. In reality, you are not being emotionally attacked and you must realize it. Tone of voice plays a major part in recovery. You know how you want someone to speak to you! Triggers from your past while in a new relationship can also bring about a cycle of abuse, because oftentimes we find ourselves comparing something minor to something major from back then.

After I left the abusive relationship, independence was very important to me. Although I was independent then, the abuser displayed a sense of control over me. Therefore, I was independent because I paid all the bills, did all the cooking, took care of the house, and was a single mom while married. I vowed not to let anyone take that type of control over me again, so when I met my current husband, it was hard for me to give up some of that power that had controlled me in the past. The kind that I promised I would never allow again. There is a difference, and it must be recognized.

I learned to give in to the love of the man that loved me back. I had to feel what was being offered as an actual gift of love, and realize it was not someone controlling me. Understanding the phases of abuse would require a strong mind, and an ability to not let my past relationship dominate my present one. After all, my feelings were always taken for granted, there was no concern for them. To feel the connection to the person God has sent me, I had to disconnect from some of the power that I said I was no longer going to give up. I had to give up some of my personal promises to obtain God's promise. This was a real moment that facing my triggers would have to find a new place in my life. I had to give up the old to obtain the new.

God had to start guiding me and ordering my steps, and I had to take my hands off of the situation. Psalm 119:133 says, *"Order my steps in thy word: and let not any iniquity have dominion over me."* This caught my attention because the definition for iniquity is wickedness or sin. Because God is ordering my steps, as long as I don't give in to the sinful nature of man, my triggers would not have dominion over me. As the new triggers came they would not have a hold on the new relationship that God sent me.

I finally had the courage to talk to the person who abused me after so many years. My triggers started activating just thinking about talking to him. It was a very difficult conversation, but it freed me from the anger that was caused, and those triggers were being released. I was able to talk about the damage that was caused, not only when in the situation, but years afterward. I also talked about the effect it had on our child. Ultimately, I unloaded all of my pain and gave it back to him. I made him feel the despair and shame that he caused. If ever given the opportunity to let the person know about how much pain they have caused, I encourage you to do so, but only if it is safe. It isn't that you need assurances of what happened, because you already know and so does the abuser. It is a step in the process of freeing yourself from the individual who had a hold over your life. I received an apology that day, and with the apology, came tears from the abuser, who asked me to forgive him. However, he did not realize that I had already forgiven him, so that I could be healed.

God says that we must forgive to be forgiven. After all, when Jesus was placed on the cross after the abuse he suffered by the hand of man, he asked God to forgive them. Luke 23:34 says, *"Father, forgive them, for they know not what they do."* Even in Jesus' darkest moment, he asked for the abusers to be forgiven. I also believe he was speaking about forgiveness of the whole world at that moment. Oftentimes, you want to forget what happened, but it causes more hurt to bury it in your mind, and it will eat at your heart. Moving forward is so important, in order to move away from whatever hurt you. It opens your heart to accept better things and allow you to move on. In order not to hold on to the pain that was caused, I had to be freed.

I must say again, this process will require us to focus on renewing the mind. It also requires a lot of study time, because it's not easy to just flip the switch of life. I now appreciate myself for recognizing the triggers and celebrate, because I can feel them for what they are in order to let them go. Doing this lets me know that part of the process of healing is taking place. Many of us find ourselves in different phases that may not have to do with a form of abuse, but coming to grips with who we are as a women, or what we want in life will require a lot of study time to reach our destinations and find our purpose. Manipulation and control should never be a part of who you grow to be.

Reflection: Phases or triggers can be your reality if you let them stop you. Gaining knowledge through them is what brings healing and takes away the challenges. Understanding your end destination once beyond them is your greatest gift.

"You used to walk in these ways, in the life you once lived. Vs 8
"But now you must also rid yourselves of all such things as these:
anger, rage, malice, slander, and filty languages from your lips."

Colossians 3:7-8(NIV)

CHAPTER 12: My Story Isn't Over

In realizing what I wanted in my life, I had to change who I had become in my past. My past played a crucial part in messing me up, both mentally and physically. I had to reevaluate myself as the beautiful woman of God who had a purpose, as He allowed me to find my voice. Women need to have a voice within a relationship, whether personal or professional. I believe what we have to add to a conversation is very important. While finding my voice, I called it a transformation. God was transforming me from the inside out, allowing me to see the beauty within. What that means is that who I had attracted in my past, was past.

I was allowed to see that my story isn't over because He is now involved. Now, this is a shouting moment because I survived! God was involved, now who can stand against Him. God had unlocked my destiny. He was the only one that held the key, because only He could see through a closed door. It was my time to grow and flourish, and all this was revealed to me beautifully. I learned to control my thoughts and words, because they attract whatever we speak. Proverbs 15:4 states, *"Gentle words bring life and health; a deceitful tongue crushes the spirit."* Think of words as being flesh, because what we speak will manifest in one form or another. God demonstrated this in the book of Genesis. You have to be intentional about who you attract in your life, and what you want. Being intentional means being in the moment. Don't even allow the weight from the past to weigh you down. Allow time to heal your wounds, no matter what they are or what caused them. Apply only positive affirmations to your life and allow them to help you heal. Pain does not always come from abuse, but it has a space in there somewhere that makes us feel lonely at times. Therefore, only reach higher and know that anything beneath does not belong to you.

Ultimately, I had to find the new me and speak the word of God over my life to attract whom God had chosen for me. Did you know that God has chosen someone for you? Trauma will have you looking for all the wrong things. We must be renewed by the word of God and filled with the sweetness of his Spirit. I had to learn to be gentle with myself, because for a while I was so fragile. Although healing did not come easily, my soul yearned for it. No written book gave me step-by-step instructions about my life and how I should prepare for it. It came to a point that I had to figure it out on my own, with God's help. Figuring life out would take time, and it came with a lot of pain.

No one else was to walk my destiny with me, it was something I had to do alone. It made me think of the Journey that Jesus took for us on the stone street in the City of Jerusalem, where they made Jesus carry the cross to his own crucifixion. Although I cannot begin to compare my journey this way, many victims of domestic violence have paved the way for us all just as Jesus did for the whole of humanity. Lives have been lost, and lessons should be learned from it. I believe that if we are paying attention, we can learn from those that have survived. However, things related to domestic violence have not changed. We are still dying! Therefore, although Jesus had a purpose to save us from our sins, what was to be my purpose? God brought me to my purpose, and he made me realize that there are so many wounds to be healed.

Many questions arose as to how I would present myself to someone that deserves the best of me. There were many issues I had to realize first. Understanding abandonment and trust from the first man that I loved was first on my list. Yes, it was my father. Who could fulfill this void I had experienced from my father? I was not looking for a replacement because God had done that himself. I had come to realize that he had taken care of the void. Secondly, moving from the stages of violence and abuse was next. This was very hard, but indeed possible. Knowing how to move forward was important, in order not to fall over any stumbling blocks that might present themselves before me. Trusting God and not my circumstances helped me evolve, and He also helped me transform into my true and divine self.

I was starting to love myself completely. Growth required getting to know me thoroughly and letting go of the woman of the past. After all, she was a woman without thought or feeling, as everything was numb to her. I thought, who am I and who do I aspire to be? I was slowly getting better at it. I was seeing what I was going to be. God was showing me that I was a woman of virtue. Have you ever looked around at the beauty of God's nature? For example, the trees that grow or the flowers that bloom.

I enjoy standing at my bedroom window while drinking a cup of coffee and watching the Glory of God outside. The beautiful, simple things. The squirrels running around playing, the birds that fly around, and the trees that stand tall in my backyard. Even a little hummingbird that comes to our window every day that I named Max. Have you ever thought about the growth of a tree and the years that it would take to reach its maturity? God revealed to me that I have to be that patient to reach the maturity that I had been created for. Also, He revealed that I had a way out of my previous relationship of abuse. When it presented itself at the beginning; I stayed. When someone shows you who they are the first time, believe them. Learn your worth and don't compromise. I learned to grow through my mistakes. Growth did not come overnight though, it matured over time like the tree, and continues to this very day.

My life was like the branches on the tree. Each growth led to brand new branches sprouting out in different directions but ultimately developing because of the life God had sustained for me. The pain that I endured because of the abuse led me to my purpose. Even in my relationship now I had to heal. Why? Because again, I could not bring my past into my present, which required maturity on my part. I also had to realize that a new relationship would bring its past as well. I understood that healing from my brokenness would take time, and you will find that out while going into your new relationship. However, you must stop and correct any mistakes immediately. Blaming others for the abuse of your past again gives your abusive partner access to your life now. It's like he's sitting right amid your home. Think about it! You might find yourself saying this is what he used to do or say to me, but now the intent behind the words is different. Let each relationship stand on its own merit, or you might find yourself alone. It is okay if that is what you choose, but if you desire to be with someone, you must move beyond your past.

You must intentionally focus on the cleansing of your soul, so to speak. I had to dig deep to remind myself of what I was trying to get away from. Was I willing to lose what God had for me based on the devil's work from my past? Absolutely not! If you put your guard up and stay in your past, then your past is where you will live. You are the one that continues to invite it in. You cannot stay in both places at the same time. Therefore, focus on today. Yesterday will be in the rearview mirror. God says to not even worry about tomorrow in scripture. In saying this, He is telling us that today is all we have, tomorrow is not promised. Unless we concentrate on the present moment, we can't give up our past, because it is in the baggage that we brought with us. Sometimes, I found a lot in my baggage, and it was heavy. In fact, it was too heavy for me to carry alone. I first had to understand the baggage that was put before me.

I had to face the fact that I carried my baggage from place to place. It came with me all the way from my youth. But how was I going to deal with it? How was I supposed to separate it? It can come in stages over the course of years. That's a whole lot of baggage, and I had to decide if it worth unpacking to fit in with my present moment. Calling on God in prayer would be the only way that I could see clearly, in order not to obscure His plan for my life. I had to remove my own baggage piece by piece to help someone else unpack theirs.

I remember my now-husband, daughter, and I relocated to another city for a job that he had obtained. There were so many boxes packed, and we had to go through each individual box, even though they were labeled, and put them in their proper place. If the box wasn't labeled correctly then it may not go into its proper place. New relationships are the same way. There is no magic to it, but true love, the love of God will enable all the baggage to be separated and put away gently in its proper place. You will find your path forward as you throw away each unpacked box that is no longer of use, or should not have been there anyway.

Therefore, like the old baggage, abuse will be a thing of the past that you put away from your present moments. You won't reflect on it, but you will allow your life to flourish in such a way that it won't take over. This is the gift of God.

It's a lesson learned in life as our steps are ordered by the Lord. When you purposely listen and know God's voice, He will reveal to you who He is and the person He has in store for you. We must listen to His voice, without allowing emotions to take control. Allow the one special person to come in and help you replace all that old baggage with something extremely beautiful. God was revealing to me the type of person that I would attract.

My field of work in nursing was my refuge and caring for others is how I survived. My patients became my family. It was there that I found who would rescue me. Once I started unpacking most of the stuff that was there, the old stuff that had to be thrown away, I began seeing a man that was different from anyone I had ever known. He had a very unique presence about himself. He also had a way of conversing that I had never experienced before, even though I had dreams of someone like him. His style was also flattering. The suits that he wore put him in a different class, and even how he looked in them was amazing to me. I also remember seeing him for the first time in a black suit and thought, "Oh my goodness, he's gorgeous!" Although I had seen individuals like this before, I thought I was out of their league. I was also not attracted to them. Why? Because they were not who God had planned for me. So, although others tried, I was not interested.

Abuse will make you think that you are not deserving of better, because your mind was held captive for so long. However, remember that God is always working. He is

121

involving you in stages that are being set, without you even knowing it. Be prepared at any time for God to work, because He will show up and show out. There was something about that particular man. Since I had seen myself only as someone who had been abused, he could not possibly be attracted to me, so I thought. I often saw myself as that person, even though I was coming out of it. I also had to remember, that person was removed with the old baggage. The way the man dressed, smiled, and walked captured my attention like no other. I thought, this is the type of person that I will attract and no longer will I attract the type of man of my past.

I did not have to do anything but be myself - my new self. You must remember I stated that the person that showed up outside of the house of abuse was that woman of beauty, she was confident and strong. It was as if my eyes were open at that very moment as I found myself worthy of better. God had opened my eyes and shown me the person He had for me. It was at a time I did not expect. We must remember that God's timing is not ours. He has our lives already planned out, and we are the ones that alter them. I called the man God had for me my Man in Black, as he rescued me. He was my superhero, without knowing his true purpose in my life.

One morning while having devotion, Pastor Touré Roberts spoke of divine nature as "God-like." He stated, "When I get a revelation of who I am, and I get a revelation of the precious promises that are over my life that can never be taken away from me, and I have come to believe it. It allows me to be transformed into my true and divine nature, which is a nature of growth, which is a nature of expansion, I can't stop it, it's natural." This has become spoken over my life, that even back then, God knew me. I had a revelation that day of who was to be in my life. My story isn't over, I thought. I had indeed transformed and attracted better. In fact, my story is still being written.

Not only had I attracted better but I attracted a Christian man. I am growing into a woman that chooses life and not death. I have become a woman that loves and will love hard. I have become a woman of virtue. I have become a woman with strategies. Yes, I have become that woman. God kept me from death, from falling into the lonely pit of darkness, and provided for me a safe haven of love. Love found me when I thought I was at my lowest point, but in reality, I wasn't. It was the beginning of my time. Do not take your old baggage with you. You must realize that old and new don't belong in the same space. See yourself as worthy of better, and when you find it, never let it go.

Each of us has a God-given destiny, and domestic abuse is not part of it. We may have simply stumbled a little, but God has picked us up to carry us the rest of the way. God gave me a vision years ago to help others going through domestic violence. I remember waking up one morning with a vision in my heart. Have you ever heard that God speaks to you in your sleep or through dreams? Psalm 16:7 states, *"I will bless the Lord who has given me counsel; my heart also instructs me in the night seasons."* When the Lord spoke to me, I felt He gave a clear message of His purpose for me. You simply have to listen to His voice. It is as if something stays with you and does not go away, until you cannot shake off what God is saying to you.

One morning on September 18, 1999, when I woke up, I heard Him loud and clear. He immediately put my purpose for my life into motion. That date coincidentally holds another special moment in my life as well. We have to be intentional about what God speaks to us about, so I got up and called a friend of mine named Cathy, to tell her about what God had revealed to me. She knew my story was God's plan put into action.

While going through an abusive relationship in my life, God kept speaking to me about a way out. Although I didn't understand it then, God gives us instructions for our lives. It is up to us to follow them. Oftentimes, we have to go through something to help someone else out of it. What this means, is that even though God gave us free will, He is there to help us when we invite Him into our lives. To help someone else we must be able to understand it ourselves. It's like education. For example, a physician cannot properly help someone if he has not received the medical experience and education to do so. Therefore, God is always ready to help us when we call on Him.

That is when I founded *A-Way-Out Ministries*. My purpose was to help others going through abusive relationships find their way out. God said to me that He was sending me back. I came to realize that he was not sending me back into the abusive relationship that once held me captive, but back to help others find a way out of theirs. Although I struggled with it at first, God had to show me that He doesn't send you on a mission alone. My test became a testimony to others that they too can survive. Although this was many years after leaving my abusive relationship, God kept speaking to me. Somehow, I did not feel I was prepared to help others because I felt I still needed help myself. I was still in the process of reliving the abuse I had experienced. I had to be nurtured by the word of God, which required lots of encouragement on my part. The old way of thinking had to be replaced by His word.

Finding peace with myself took one day at a time. I remember going to someone's home who had just lost her daughter and grandchild to domestic violence. The fact that she heard the shots without realizing that it was her family losing their life, gave me a fearful feeling. Her daughter lived in an apartment slightly behind her. I remember going to speak to this woman to assist her with her needs because of the loss. I found myself reliving my own situation, and many triggers hit me all at once, because so many victims were still losing their lives. I began to question God as to how I can be the one to help someone else, when I still needed help myself. It was a process to get to a place of helping others.

I also remember my organization helping a family that lost their loved one that was killed violently. It was horrible. I started to experience triggers through what I heard of others' pain. Triggers would sometimes come and send my mind into a very dark place. I hadn't ever told my story completely, only small parts of it. I couldn't bring myself to let people know that I allowed someone to treat me that way. After all, I viewed myself as an independent, strong, fearless woman. Outside those doors of abuse, this was how I was perceived. Many people that have known me for years didn't know that I held an awful secret. I am sure that many people have also experienced abuse but will not admit to it and will instead live in silence with their past.

I was at this event one day for women entrepreneurs, and I met a gentleman by the name of Maurice Carter. He came up to me and introduced himself at our booth that we had set up. He was excited to run into someone that spoke about domestic violence, and he spoke to me about his purpose relative to it. I believe that there is a reason and a season for people to either enter or exit our lives, and this was his season. I had my organization *A-Way-Out* on display for domestic violence in the midst of many women vendors, many other vendors there were just selling merchandise. We connected, he shared his story, and I spoke of mine in the short version. We exchanged information and once we finally had the opportunity to sit down and talk, he explained his purpose to me.

He had wonderful ideas of what he wanted for his media company, BBP, to form a partnership with my organization. I received wonderful video footage of other stories that he had covered from his media company, and he told me we could plan to do some film work together. After our first meeting, it was decided that he wanted to film me interviewing someone that had experienced domestic violence. It was very important to him that people experiencing domestic violence find a safe way out. I agreed and was very excited about our partnership.

Later, a thought had entered my mind, but I kind of shoved it off. The thought kept coming back to me, and I was like God is this you? Indeed, it was. He was telling me to have Maurice interview me instead of me interviewing someone else about my story of abuse. Was this why God sent him my way? After all, this wasn't the understanding that Maurice and I had. After careful thought, and much hesitation, I spoke to my husband about telling my own story instead of Maurice interviewing me with someone else. Now because I had never told my entire story, the thought of it was frightening. Could this be the healing that I needed, and was Maurice the person being used to do it? To my surprise, my husband was open to the idea and felt it could be healing for me. I decided to run the idea by Maurice, and he grabbed onto it right away. He understood my hesitancy though in putting my story out. He also understood the stigma of shame that I felt once it was released, but he encouraged me as well. This was my time.

We set up a day for filming, and now my story is on YouTube. Maurice helped me work through my hesitancy by reminding me it would help someone else. I felt a sense of freedom after completing the filming, like was some type of release. For the first time, I had shared my entire story. It was a story that not one person outside myself knew the entirety of. However, something kept bothering me about how people would view me. Guilt and shame tried to show up again as my story was to be released. Should I really share my story? The thought of it terrified me. I would be revealing my past to all the people in my life who did not know my story, and those that knew my past did not know the full extent of it. I pondered whether to advertise its existence on YouTube.

However, God kept tugging at me to not worry about what other people thought about me. The stigma of shame stays with you forever if you don't release it. After all, none of the people I was concerned about had any impact on my life. I was in a judgement-free zone with God, so their thoughts of me could not take away my new life. God told me to keep my mind focused on Him. Maurice said that it is time to help those that are experiencing the same type of abuse and be the voice that would let someone else know that there is a way out. Once Maurice sent me the video, I was still somehow nervous and frightened. I took my mind off of God and focused on the situation.

Again, I shared my thoughts with my husband, and even shared with my daughter how I felt about its release. I also felt I needed my daughter's permission to share this story because she was a major part of it even though she knew I was doing the interview. I had to make her aware the project was ready for release. Receiving her permission to release it lifted a huge burden from my heart, she helped me feel free and unashamed in that moment. I also sent the actual YouTube video story to my friend Nicole and a few others before sharing it with friends and family on social media. Nicole sent me feedback that further affirmed that I needed to share my story.

She told me that sharing has the power to remove guilt and shame, as the enemy tries to tell us that somehow what happened to us was our fault. She also said it also serves as tangible evidence for the woman still going through abuse that there is a way out! They might connect in a new way as they hear their own stories coming from someone else's mouth. Nicole added that my testimony would be the light in someone else's path. It was Maurice, Nicole, my husband, and my daughter, Rikita that helped me through the shame. By taking me outside the stigma that was attached to my story of abuse, God gave me my voice. He had already provided the open door for me. He said that because my story had already been written, I can't decide to alter what had happened. It's like altering the path of Jesus. Shame can't come from what will provide freedom for others. I am free to walk in my purpose, and walk away from shame, because it no longer belongs to me. It is important to move towards my mission. God will remove any obstacles in your way, before you even get started on your journey.

Now came time to face my fears, and let people know why I started my organization. God also revealed to me that the ministry wasn't just my organization, it was my purpose. The real reason behind the organization was my survival to push past the stigma that is attached to people that have been abused. The reason was for others to learn that someone understands how they feel, and God is revealing to them that there is a way out. I posted the video on social media and let it go. And I felt peace about it. Like David, in the bible, I was able to slay my giant, and God prepared me for the rest that would come. I understand that I am here to help others try and reconcile the tragedy in their lives through the trauma that they have experienced. This healing journey will take time, but God will give us the strength to walk through our valleys together, and that mountain shall come down.

I am a living witness that God can take your giants, your mountains, and pain whatever it might be, and turn it into purpose. However, in finding my purpose, I had to let go of people that did not bring value to my life. I realized that not everyone was meant to be in this season of my life. I simply removed myself, and I am good with that. No longer am I going to allow others to dictate the life that God has given me. I have accepted that part of their story is over, and no longer will they be able to add a new chapter to my life. I've learned to march to my own beat, without worrying about the acceptance of others.

Reflection: Seasons will come in our lives when life changes along the way. If we learn through them, we can accept them as part of our growth. Reevaluating your journey can help you accept the path ahead.

"For I know the plans I have for you," declares the Lord, "plans to prosper you and not to harm you, plans to give you hope and a future."

Jeremiah 29:11 (NIV)

Daisy Arness Marrs

CHAPTER 13: A Woman No Longer Deceived
(Woman Thou Art Loosed)

I remember Bishop T.D Jakes's book called *Woman Thou Art Loosed*. What did that mean for me? How much trauma have I experienced from abuse that I didn't feel free? How much am I still holding onto? I often wondered if the wounds of my past could be healed. How can I be loosened from the abuse and no longer deceived by evil? Being "loosed" to me meant more than what the title was saying. During the times that I was being abused, there was no one telling me what I could be. What was I to be loosed from? I thought I was stuck in an unchanging situation. There is a season outside of our pain that is waiting for us. It is already here because we have survived and are moving forward in our purpose. We have moved beyond our circumstances and buried them. We have become women who are stronger, wiser, and have gained an impactful vision of ourselves. We can find new relationships that we can build upon, because we know our boundaries and limitations. Learn what it is that you now cherish about yourself, and never let anyone take it away. Don't be deceived by the naysayers who refuse to admit what they went through.

Regaining your identity allows you to seek someone deserving of you. You are a woman that has been loosed from the abuse that held you in bondage. Therefore, it will help reveal the negative energy that once attracted you. I found that I have favor from God, because of the life He has for me. I also learned that leaving the situation provided a space of opportunity to redevelop myself. God's word challenged me to go beyond my expectations. The ability to walk beyond toxic relationships was greater than just me, it was because I had a higher calling in my life. I had to learn when God says move, I must move, and leave nothing undone. I challenge you to do the same.

I am also always building my daughter up through the word of God. I am nobody without Him, so how can my advice alone be good for her? I have to pray about what it is God has for her and her family's life, because without Him I can't give her clear direction. I have to pray over her circumstance, whatever it is, and direct her accordingly. God's word and His promises are powerful, and anyone can tap into them. You too will be placed in a position that has you motivated to get to your next level, and nothing can stop you. I had to realize that it wasn't about the house I bought or the furniture that was left inside, it was never mine anyway. When you leave this earth there is absolutely nothing that will go with you. None of the material things that I had protected me, not even the closed doors that were attached to the house kept me safe. They provided me with an exit, but it was an entrance for the person that tried to take my life. God said there is provision over your life, and the vision is even more than you can hold. God said, "Go", and I went.

Learning that I was called to go back to help others that were being abused meant I now have a purpose. Basically, because I am now a living testimony, I can help someone else survive and find shelter through their storm. Pastor Sarah Roberts said that God promised there is going to come a time when you are positioned properly, and that is when you will have the ultimate fulfillment because you can find yourself where you are supposed to be. When you're not who you are supposed to be, you feel unfilled. While helping others find a way out of their toxic environment, I am at the same time fulfilled in the work that I'm doing. It's like setting the captives free. Isaiah 61:1 says, *"The Spirit of the Sovereign Lord is on me because the Lord has anointed me to proclaim good news to the poor; He has sent me to bind up the brokenhearted, to proclaim freedom for the captives and release from darkness for the prisoners."*

No matter how uncomfortable I am in returning to places of trauma, I must go back and let abuse know it does not have control over me. All the stages of abuse that I left behind were only preparing me for greater things. I had to return to the place of unfulfillment to be fulfilled. I can now stand up against the hell that had a hold on me and stand face to face with it. My voice is being heard, and my peace is being fulfilled. God is taking me back, but He is with me. I am not alone in the midst of the storm.

There are many circumstances that may have a hold on you, but God didn't allow them to take you down. When He sent me to a place of peace and brought the person in my life that he had for me, chains were broken. My vision became emboldened. Being able to overcome the torment and fears that had attached themselves to me, is no longer part of my story. I have been given a new story that is filled with love. I am a woman that is no longer deceived and have now been loosed from the torment of hell. No longer are we to be struck down by the words of man, and those things that took you to a place of deception can no longer hold you. God said I have given you victory over the territories of your life. Hallelujah! It is shouting time! I am no longer bound by the demonic spirits that once had a hold on me.

I can now face the situations I once feared and let all the stigmas attached to them go. I am built for better. I walk differently because God is protecting me. My destiny has been redirected and now the attacks can't touch me. My preparation for life has steered me into a direction that is only obtainable through the truth. My influence on others will have a positive impact so they can obtain what God has for them in their life. In order to do this, I can't be deceived by someone that has no purpose for my life. I need someone who will not allow me to fall. Going back to school for Christian Ministry and obtaining my degree also allows me to help others that are searching for a relationship with God. I have to be connected to the word of God in such a way that it is ingrained in my heart and part of my soul.

Building upon the good that's inside of me will protect me from all the shame life has tried to place on me. 1 Corinthians 15:33 says, *"Be not deceived: evil communications corrupt good manners."* What God is telling me from this verse is that I can't be around bad company and produce good fruit. Pick apart those that question His authority and release them to go on their way if they are not willing to listen. Questioning His word over my life isn't what brings peace, it is His peace that gives me life. I also must choose my battles and be vigilant to my surroundings. I must closely monitor those that come into my space, because everyone was not built to be there. Be mindful when God has given you directions to work towards beneficial people.

God reminds me that in every situation I have experienced He was there with me. As tears were falling, He was there to wipe them away. He does not leave us alone in the midst of the storms of life. God gives us strength to endure every situation that impacts us, like in birth when you can't see past the pain of the present moment, after it's all over the pain subsides. As women, we refuse to keep losing as we learn that we are not fighting this life alone.

1 Samuel 17:47 says, *"All those gathered here will know that it is not by sword or spear that the Lord saves; for the battle is the Lord's, and he will give all of you into our hands."* This tells me God will deliver me, and that whoever is trying to harm me must stand against the Lord, because I am not alone in this battle. Although challenges of life will come, I am building myself up for the better part of me that can withstand the hard

times. Moments of deception will creep up on you, as they have me, and being prepared takes more than saying "I am ready." My life required strength, endurance, and pushing through the pain while preventing myself from getting lost in the dark times. Finding my voice has made me a champion over my own self.

Your voice is the most powerful tool you have. As walls sometimes seem too high to climb, there is a space between them that you can shimmy through in order to propel yourself upwards, and once you are there scream loudly and boldly. So, take hold of that moment and just breathe. Breathing allows me to accept my present moment one breath at a time. I am living a real-life story, not a dream that belonged to someone else. I can create my own story and find joy in doing so. I no longer give anyone permission to write my story and if they tried, their pages would simply be blank. Have you ever wondered why you thought that someone else had it all together only to later find out they did not? Nobody on this earth has it all together, so beating up on myself became a thing of the past. When I introduce myself, I do it boldly. I pronounce every letter of my name because I am *somebody*. My name means something, and it stands for me.

I am given clarity on what happiness is and how to obtain it. Scripture says in Matthew 6:33, *"But seek first the Kingdom of God, and his righteousness; and all these things shall be added to you."* The word of God didn't say "maybe" or "if," it said, "shall be added." As long as I pray before I do anything, and trust and believe in His word, God is right there. That is His promise. God has given me a gift to serve others, so how can I do it if I am not being served?

Did you know that forgiveness plays a huge part in moving forward? Forgiving others is essential in order to obtain the grace of God to come out from under the shell hiding you from them. Living beyond my yesteryears required a huge leap of faith. The ache that caused me to not move forward was gone, and my breakthrough was coming. Opportunities that did not seem to exist were there all along and grabbing them was just an itch away. I was walking with a new glow, because the dullness that dimmed my light did not have a hold on me any longer. I became comfortable in my own skin, the beautiful light-skinned girl that was rejected by my father. Do you know how that feels? How awesome it was to visualize that moment when I realized someone else couldn't knock the wind out of me after all. You are able to rise above the abuse and realize that you are a woman that has been loosed. Deception is a thing of the past and choosing to condemn those that don't belong in your space is the freedom that took me a while to get to.

Sharing my space now requires big shoes to fill because of God as he has shown me my worth. The man God has given me has helped me find my voice as well. To fix a heart that was once broken is difficult in so many ways, because there are so many tiny pieces to put back together. I now know that the part of my heart that needed fixing was its capability for attachment. He has connected it in such a way that every chamber within it now flows freely. As we know nothing broken can survive, and every puzzle has a piece that connects it for completion, if one piece is out of place then the picture is incomplete.

Just as God made Eve for Adam according to Genesis 2:7, I believe that everyone has someone made especially for them. It may take a while to find them, but they are there. My husband now adds to my completion, my assignment, and he has given me the freedom to be who God created me to be. There are no hidden agendas, and that is simply amazing. In realizing that deception is from the devil, God will guide your heart if you allow him to. James 4:7 tells us to *"Submit yourselves, then, to God. Resist the devil, and he will flee."* You may find yourself asking, how can I resist the devil when he is always present trying to take what belongs to me? Ephesians 6:11 says, *"Put on the full armor of God so that you can take your stand against the devil's schemes."* God's word tells us that the devil will be working against us, trying to make us fall. However, He gives us protection from the devil that will help us win the fight to keep our peace.

Learning the tricks of the devil are key to following the path that God has for us. Although I have stumbled many times, the word of God has helped me get right back up. He is ever-present in my time of need and quickens my heart to let me know He is there. Having a personal conversation with God also helps me know the deception that the devil tries to send towards me. The devil hates when I have those conversations with God, especially during my praise and worship moments. I allow myself to enter into the space with God. Tears flow, rejoicing happens, and then my peace comes. Know that it is okay to put on your dancing shoes and move about freely in the presence of God. Enemies will continue trying to deceive you but listening to the music of your dance will guide you through.

God's direction will always steer us to a safe place. Staying focused to be held accountable is more important than ever. Accountability shifts us to righteousness and fixes our wrongs. Immediate gratification comes from acknowledging all of this. I make no apologies for wanting to change what has already been written in my life but recognizing it instead of painting a different picture, brings my reality into display. Indeed, being deceived is no longer an option because I am always vigilant, even to those that choose not to know me. I pray for them.

Reflection: Freedom can bring changes, but not knowing will hold you back. Once you realize who you have become then nothing in life can hold you back.

"Beloved, do not believe every spirit, but test the spirits to see whether they are from God, for many false prophets have gone out into the world."

1 John 4:1 ESV

CHAPTER 14: Driven By Purpose

I have come to realize that once I understood what was defining me, I understood I must have a purpose. But then came more questions. What is my purpose here on earth? Was abuse part of my purpose? While these are questions I cannot definitively answer, I am driven by purpose now. Although we can't see what it is, we must figure it out. Little by little, it will come to pass. However, we cannot do this by ourselves. I believe that God shows us our purpose through little snippets throughout our life. I often can look back and see them. Sometimes insecurities that we may have such as fear, low self-esteem, and lack of confidence can alter our purpose. Therefore, discovering how to conquer all these things can lead us to our path of righteousness. If we don't realize our insecurities, something meant to come our way could be altered. The more snippets that show up, the closer we are to finding purpose.

I stated in an earlier chapter that domestic violence was not supposed to define me. It was not my purpose to stay in it, but to help someone else out of it. I also believe that once we don't see the negative signs that are displayed immediately in front of us, our purpose can be redefined. I did this for a long time, because I was allowing other people's thoughts of me to alter my purpose. I asked, was my abuse a part of the plan? I realize that one of the most important things in my life was re-establishing myself. I had to find the reason behind it. What can I change in my life to get me back on track in finding my purpose? What is it that I am supposed to pay particular attention to? I can honestly say now that it does not involve what others may think of me. At first, I thought it did, especially if they chose not to be a part of my life.

Ask yourself a simple question. After leaving the abuse of your past, why are you willing to let anyone else keep you there? That means they are judging you. I always thought about how others viewed what I was doing, what I posted on social media, what I said, or how I carried myself. Even down to the decisions I made, I was concerned of how people viewed me. I allowed other people's views and thoughts of me to alter my path. I was placing myself back in the past as someone that was being affected mentally. Mental abuse can keep you in a dark place for as long as you allow it. I will not allow it any longer. It will also allow them to dictate your life, instead of you taking charge. This should never become who you are. Judgment from others should not define us, because only the judgment of God is all that matters.

Love should not hurt in any form. If anyone brings you pain, or any type of mental anguish, then they have shown that they don't really want to be a part of your life. They have simply created their own narrative, and who you are isn't important to them. For instance, I have given myself permission to move on. We will all be judged one day, and that will be our ultimate journey with God. For now, judgment from others does not outweigh God's purpose for our lives.

I found my dream of becoming a nurse so real that I couldn't let what people thought about me failing the first time alter my path. Becoming a nurse is what drove me and working as a rehabilitation nurse was most important. They were the ones that needed the most fixing or help. It was important to me that I help them get back to their best self. It allowed me to show love to the people that were in my care and helped me to care for them by assisting during their healing. All of that helped me as well. As a nurse, we make plans for our patients to assist them in their care needs properly. This requires a team of people in assisting the patient to reach their maximum goal before discharge from the hospital or rehabilitation center. This is a medical plan put in place from admission to the facility that will help medical staff with the care of patients put in their care. If we put this same type of plan in action while determining our life's planning, then it will be beneficial in finding purpose.

Start from the beginning of your understanding of life and plan from there, almost like setting goals for yourself. Separating what is not providing for us with what may be helpful can provide us with structure while transitioning. Taking time to figure out the reasons behind the choices that we made, could be our path to finding our true selves. How much time was wasted living someone else's life? The abuse took away so much from me, so how much more was I willing to give up? Finding out that you cannot be caught within a trap by someone else's doing will prevent you from wasting your time. There are tons of opportunities and gifts that God has given each of us, and the opinions of others should not be part of it. To find purpose, we each have been given an inner desire. We must dig deep, and some may have to dig even deeper than others, but what God has for us is there.

Continuing the nurse analogy to illustrate purpose, many are in it simply for the pay rather than the patient. It is not their purpose. A purpose makes you present in the moment and different from others that may occupy the same space. They show up to the job to earn a paycheck. They may not be totally attentive to the care of people that are in their care. Purpose is why you show up and put every bit of you into caring for the people that you have responsibility for. My heart's desire for nursing is what makes me uniquely different from the person who goes into it just to make a living.

Remember when I spoke of dreaming as a young child about my desire to become a nurse? Helping others was so important to me. It was so important that I did not give up on obtaining my nursing license, even when in an abusive relationship. I learned that the abusive relationship did not switch up my purpose to become a nurse, because as a survivor I was able to give compassion to those in my care who had experienced abuse. I felt their pain, even if it didn't have to deal with domestic violence. There were times when it did, but it was the strong desire to help in any way I could that gave me purpose as a nurse. Was that my assignment here on earth? I believe what we experience personally in our lives allows us to have compassion for others that have experienced the same thing, but it goes even beyond that.

Let's think of it this way, Jesus came to earth for the purpose of saving us because of sin. God and sin cannot dwell in the same space. I learned in my studies that for a brief moment, Jesus was actually separated from God because he took on sin for everyone. Once Jesus died to sin, He was resurrected. Therefore, after defeating sin, he was no longer separated from God. While on earth, Jesus healed, saved people, and performed miracles. He also served his purpose before his walk on earth was over. It is the same for us. Our purpose has many channels to it, but ultimately one, and we too are separated from God until we accept Him as our Lord and Savior by asking forgiveness of our sins.

I was also able to be a counselor, and a prayer warrior in times of need. While holding hands with others through their tears, I was able to be there for them through their fears. Our purpose will serve others, that's what we are here for. If we think that the assignment has changed, it has only shifted.

Did you know that staying in an abusive relationship keeps you from your purpose? Do you understand that the person doing the abusing is manipulating you to serve them instead? Although I am not professionally educated in this area, I had to learn this through my studies of God's word. While I was being abused, my assignment in life couldn't be fulfilled because I was living a purpose that someone else had for me. If you are living someone else's life you can't be living your own. Ultimately, I understood that the longer I stayed the longer it took me to get where I should be in life.

Establishing your now is what will draw you to your purpose. While in that relationship you ignored your own dreams because you were afraid or prevented from fulfilling them. You couldn't follow your purpose due to the hold the abusive person had on you. By going back to nursing school, I was fulfilling the desire of my heart, but it wasn't until I left the abuse that I fulfilled it as stated in the previous chapter. However, my abuser was not able to receive any benefit from my God-given purpose as a nurse. Therefore, it is not too late to prove that you are necessary in this world in order to reach your goals. I have become intentional in what God shows me. Whatever God gives brings me peace, and whatever He doesn't bring is chaos. It is just that simple.

When it is time to remove yourself, do not think twice about it. The attention is being taken away from your purpose, and when the direction shifts away from what drives you, the devil takes the opportunity to step in and cause conflict. God does not provide conflict. Ultimately, whatever we shift our minds toward, God will steer us in the right direction.

Remember to wear your God-given armor. By allowing yourself to discover your purpose, you will find that God is shielding you. Have you ever realized that when choosing God over your enemies, He will keep you from unnecessary circumstances that try to distract you? There are so many things or people in this world that can bring heartache, but the word of God shows us that we are more than our circumstances.

While doing devotion one morning I came across a statement by Samuel Rutherford that said, "After winter comes the summer. After night comes the dawn. And after every storm, there come clear, open skies." As simple as this statement is, it speaks volumes. This speaks to the seasons in our lives as I spoke of in an earlier chapter. It was extremely hard to weather the storm that I endured. Looking back on it I don't know how I survived it in my natural mind. I lived through a real horror story. However, Jesus was an example that there is purpose through them if we succeed. Jesus knew he would make it to his purpose because of His Father's plan for his life. He also knew that God was with him, as he had to withstand all the obstacles that stood in his way to allow the purpose of God for his life to be fulfilled. That is what we are to do to receive what God has for us.

Just as it wasn't easy for Jesus when he walked the earth, it will not be for us. 1 Peter 1:7 says, *"These trials are only to test your faith, to see whether or not it is strong and pure."* Although I had to endure the test and learn through it to find God, I must admit the test was a hard one. Yes, it was extremely hard. Although I did not know what the outcome would be, I realize that what we go through in life makes us stronger, and we can help someone else through it. After all, people that have not been on a journey such as ours could never understand what it took to endure something so intense. They can assist with needs but ultimately, they can't understand our passion for it. It is simply not their purpose. Passion will drive you while you fulfill your purpose.

Oftentimes I found myself reaching for something that I did not already know I had. The feeling of abandonment made me feel as though I was not loved, and because I did not understand that there was a higher power already working in my life, I was left shattered for a long time. Learning early in life about who you are will help you walk into your purpose. In addition, we must learn that no one is allowed to have power or control over us under any circumstance. Choosing yourself over the power of others will help cut abuse off at its roots. Become proud of who you are, and don't let anyone take you for granted. When you do soul searching and find things that you are not happy with, change them immediately. I was not happy with the way my life turned out because from the start there was discomfort.

My happiness today does not come from someone else. You simply can't survive on that alone. Don't get me wrong, others add to our lives, but they cannot sustain us on their own. Think of the millionaires of the world and the riches that they hold. They should be happy, shouldn't they? Yet you still find them committing suicide, going through a divorce, or simply not happy in their own skin. Ultimately, money will not sustain you either. Although it will help make the journey easier it will not bring you complete happiness. It does not come from the outside or in what we obtain, it comes from the God within and the love that we find in ourselves.

Have you ever been told by someone that they love you? Of course, you have. How did it make you feel when they disappointed you? Loving yourself and finding peace within yourself will give you the ability to deal with letdowns. We are loved unconditionally by God, and that means all of us. After all, He sent His son Jesus to save us. Now that's love. He literally died for us. However, the love of man will let you down every time, so don't place high expectations on them. Their love often comes with stipulations such as, "I love you if, I love you because, I love you for, or I love you when." There are many more I am sure we all have heard before. We barely hear "I love just for being who you are. Who God actually created you to be." Just like love may come in different stages, so will our purpose.

There is so much power in our purpose because of God. We have to learn that as much as we are driven by purpose, we must not reach for levels that are not within our reach yet. What this meant for me, is because I was in a stage of abuse in my life, my purpose was not within my reach when I let someone else control it. A tight grip was held on my dream of becoming a nurse, and I could not reach it yet. Once out of the abusive situation, I was finally starting to fix and repair myself, so my purpose was more reachable. I was trying to revive myself and get myself together. Revision allowed me to start walking towards and eventually into my purpose and my dream.

Although the stage of my dreams was being set, other things had to come into play. It did not take me long to figure out that I could not have a mess and purpose at the same time. I was still a mess, and I was trying to find out who I was in Christ while coming out of the devil's den. Who knew that life could be such a challenge? The devil thought he had me, but God said, not this one. Staying in an abusive relationship will cause you to abandon or delay your stages of life that lead you to your purpose. After all, it started out in my youth and continued into adulthood. Many years of what could have been, was not because of it. Was this time wasted? I don't know, but I thank God for keeping me.

Breaking the cycle of abuse is essential in knowing who you are very early in life. Don't allow what you see to become who you are. Generational curses can be broken, because you don't have to be a product of your past. Ultimately, life and all that it has to offer is waiting for you to start your new journey. Walk peacefully into your purpose. Be bold about it, move forward without fear, and you will allow doors to open that you never knew were there. They will open for you just as they will for others as you help them along the way.

It will also allow you to invite in the people that God had waiting for you all along. Your voice will be heard, so speak loud and clear. Be brave, be intentional, be driven, but above all be free.

Reflection: For every season there must be a purpose, and for every purpose, there must be a season. People change as seasons change. Don't get caught up in the uncertainty of change. We must not allow people to alter our purpose. Staying focused will help guide you to the direction intended and shape you into your God-given purpose.

"I Cry out to God Most High, to God, who fulfills his purpose for me."

Psalm 57:2 (ESV)

ABOUT THE AUTHOR
DAISY ARNESS MARRS

D aisy Marrs has been a nurse for over thirty years in which she found healing through helping others. She also obtained her Cosmetology License in 1986 and opened up a Hair Salon in 1999 called *Fashions Hair Designs*. As God spoke to her, He informed her that He was sending her back to help others experiencing abuse, to find their way out. It was then, He gave her the vision to help others going through domestic violence and *A-Way-Out Ministries* was founded in 1999. Daisy also recorded a gospel CD in support of the organization. She received her degree in Christian Ministry from Indiana Wesleyan University in the year 2020 to let others know that God has a purpose for their lives and abuse is not part of it. It is important to her that victims find a way out of abusive relationships and enjoy life on the other side of abuse. You can find her story *"Domestic Terror The Daisy Marrs Story"* on YouTube.

"Understanding the phases of abuse would require a strong mind to not let your past relationship dominate your present one."

— *Daisy Marrs*

"Finding yourself is more powerful than life itself because it is then that you have found home."

— *Daisy Marrs*

A-WAY-OUT MINISTRIES

A-Way-Out Ministries Inc. is a 501c3 nonprofit organization established in 1999 as a means of providing support to women and children who are going through periods of crisis due to domestic violence in the home or in the community. This support includes education, awareness, and prevention through workshops, partnerships, speaking engagements at churches, schools, and wherever support is needed.   We partner with   other   organizations that specialize in programs to help those at risk and need a way out of violent or unhealthy relationships.

Address: 7999 Shadeland Ave. Suite 230 Indianapolis, Indiana 46350

Website: www.a-way-outministries.org

Phone Number 317-676-5021

If you have an emergency to report, either for yourself or on behalf of someone who is close to you, please call 9-1-1 in the state in which you reside. You can also Call the National Domestic Violence hotline number at 1-800-799-7233.

For Immediate emergency assistance please call your local 911 emergency system right away.

Denola M. Burton
www.EnhancedDNAPublishing.com
DenolaBurton@EnhancedDNA1.com